YOU GET SOMETHING EXTRA FROM EVERYTHING ARMOUR

ARMOUR

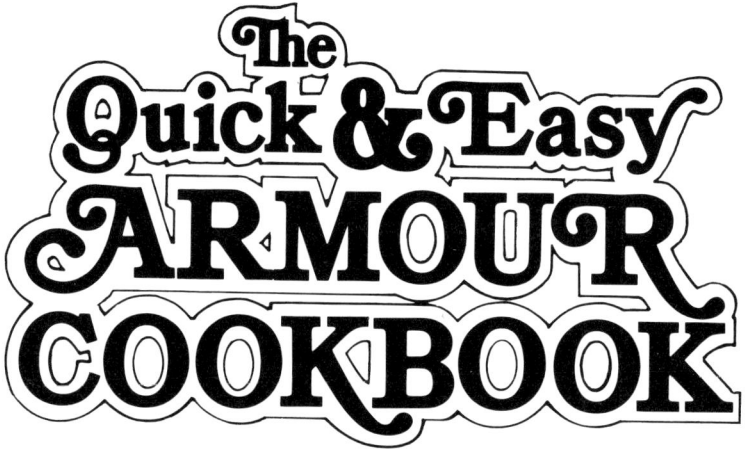

A Benjamin Company/Rutledge Book

All the recipes in this cookbook were developed and tested by home economists in the Armour and Company kitchens.

Photography by Gordon E. Smith

*Copyright © 1980 by Armour and Company.
All rights reserved.*

*Prepared and produced by Rutledge Books, Inc.
 25 W. 43 Street, New York, N.Y. 10036*

*Published by The Benjamin Company, Inc.
 485 Madison Avenue, New York, N.Y. 10022*

Library of Congress Catalog Card Number: 80-66316
ISBN: 0-87502-082-8
Printed in the United States of America
First Printing: June, 1980

The following are registered trademarks of Armour and Company: Armour, Armour Star, Golden Star, Appian Way, Treet, Caserta, Veribest.

Contents

A Cookbook for Today	6
Turkey Talk	8
Ham Facts	9
Breakfast & Brunch	10
Appetizers & Snacks	26
Lunches	48
Main Dishes	96
Company's Coming	136
Index	156

A Cookbook for Today

George Bernard Shaw once wrote, "There is no love sincerer than the love of food."

At Armour, we'd like to exercise poetic license and update the great author's sentiment: "There is no love sincerer than the love of *convenient, easy to prepare food.*" And in this special cookbook, you'll find that every Armour product and recipe is designed to provide you wholesome, delicious *and* convenient meals that reflect today's exciting and fast-paced lifestyles.

It's true that, over the years, hundreds of thousands of recipes, many of them now familiar classics in American homes, have been created and tested in the Armour kitchens. But did you know that Armour and Company played a major role in the very evolution of today's food technology?

When Armour first began operations in 1867, salt cure was the sole means by which fresh meat products were preserved. Only seven years later—in a move that would change the food industry forever—Armour built, in its Chicago plant, the world's first "chill room," the forerunner of refrigerators and freezers. By 1878, just nine years after the last spike was driven in the transcontinental railroad, Armour was operating its own refrigerated railroad cars.

By the late 1880s, Armour was also among the pioneers of canned food production. By the turn of the century, Armour's reputation for top-quality processed meat products was a byword with consumers across the nation.

These technological milestones marked the conversion of meat processing from a seasonal business to an annual one. Thus, for the first time, Americans had access to meat products, both fresh and processed, all year 'round—a convenience we take for granted today.

The Armour philosophy, one which has endured for more than a century, was expressed by J. Ogden Armour (son of Philip D. Armour, company founder) in his 1917 "Description of Business": "Our business is to gather up the nation's perishable food products, carefully preserve their taste, texture and nutritional qualities, standardize them for convenience and then distribute them throughout the world."

By both developing and drawing on the technology of each succeeding decade, Armour has been at the leading edge of many giant advances in food preparation, from instant, canned and frozen to dehydrated and freeze-dried.

At Armour, products and processes are continually being developed and improved upon by our highly skilled staff of scientists who work in one of the industry's most advanced research laboratories—Armour's Research and Development Lab in Scottsdale, Arizona. But it is our home economists who give personality and artistry to food technology. They are the ones who develop and test products to ultimately provide the vast array of creative recipes that you have come to treasure.

The recipes in this cookbook have been thoughtfully and carefully chosen for their quality, taste, appearance, ease of preparation and overall convenience. We organized them into five helpful meal-planning chapters. Each delicious dish was tested and retested before it was finally selected to appear among the more than 200 that we've compiled. The 32 beautiful color photographs will show you some of the irresistible results. And where appropriate, microwave instructions are included.

Over the years, our recipes have been updated and adapted as new appliances, new products and new technologies have demanded it. But certain elements never change—Armour products and recipes are traditionally nutritious, imaginative, practical and convenient. We are confident that Armour products and recipes in this special cookbook will save you time and effort—and reward you with delicious dishes you'll want to make again and again.

Happy cooking—from Armour.

TURKEY TALK

Yield
When buying turkeys weighing 12 pounds and under, allow ¾ to 1 pound (raw weight) per serving. For turkeys weighing over 12 pounds, allow ½ to ¾ pound (raw weight) per serving.

Thawing
To thaw a frozen turkey, place on tray in refrigerator for the time specified in chart below. For quicker thawing, use a combination method: Set the turkey out at room temperature, then refrigerate it.

THAWING GUIDE FOR FROZEN TURKEYS

WEIGHT	REFRIGERATOR	COMBINATION (Room Temperature + Refrigerator)
4-8 lbs.	1-2 days	6 hours + 12 hours
8-12 lbs.	2 days	7 hours + 12 hours
12-16 lbs.	2-3 days	8 hours + 12 hours
16-20 lbs.	3 days	10 hours + 12 hours
20-24 lbs.	3-4 days	12 hours + 12 hours

Roasting
Turkeys should be roasted at 325°F. for times indicated on the following chart. When a meat thermometer, inserted in the center of the thigh and not touching the bone, registers 180°F., the turkey is done. If the turkey is roasted unstuffed, decrease roasting time by approximately 30 minutes. Complete preparation and roasting instructions are on the labels of all Armour turkeys.

ROASTING CHART

WEIGHT	UNCOVERED PAN 325°F. OVEN
4-6 lbs.	2 - 2½ hours
6-8 lbs.	2½ - 3 hours
8-10 lbs.	3 - 3½ hours
10-12 lbs.	3½ - 4 hours
12-14 lbs.	4 - 4½ hours
14-16 lbs.	4½ - 5 hours
16-18 lbs.	5 - 5¼ hours
18-20 lbs.	5¼ - 5½ hours
20-22 lbs.	5½ - 5¾ hours
22-24 lbs.	5¾ - 6 hours

Boneless Turkeys

The Armour Golden Star Boneless Young Turkey is the same high quality Armour turkey, butter basted and easy to slice, but without the bones. It has the natural proportion of white and dark meat along with outside skin to allow for browning. When purchasing the boneless turkey, allow approximately 6 ounces (raw weight) per serving.

Thawing

To thaw a boneless turkey, place in plastic wrapper on a tray in refrigerator for 2 to 3 days.

Roasting

A boneless turkey should be roasted at 350°F. for the times indicated in the chart below. The turkey is done when a meat thermometer registers 170-175°F. Complete oven roasting, covered and rotisserie grill, and microwave instructions are on the label of the Armour Golden Star Boneless Young Turkey.

ROASTING CHART FOR BONELESS TURKEYS

WEIGHT	OVEN ROAST AT 350°F.
2-4 lbs.	2½ to 3 hrs.
4-6 lbs.	3 to 3½ hrs.
6-8 lbs.	3½ to 4 hrs.

HAM FACTS

Basically, there are three popular types of hams found in the supermarket: fully cooked, boneless hams that have been canned for preservation; fully cooked, boneless hams that are sealed in a plastic bag to keep their freshness; and bone-in hams.

A general guide for buying and serving boneless ham is to allow ¼ to ⅓ pound per serving. The label will give specific heating instructions for each product. In general, a fully cooked ham can be served cold, or heated to an internal temperature of 140° in a 325° oven, 20 to 25 minutes per pound.

Canned hams are processed to pasteurization temperature and require refrigeration. Vacuum sealed in metal or plastic containers, canned hams may be refrigerated *unopened* up to 12 months. Once opened, tightly wrap unused portion in plastic wrap; refrigerate up to one week. Freezing is not recommended as it causes flavor and texture changes.

Ham is high in nutritive value, an excellent source of protein, B vitamins and minerals. Available in numerous styles, shapes and sizes, ham is easy to prepare and versatile for use in many types of recipes.

Breakfast & Brunch

With Armour products, every breakfast can be "over-easy"! Here are two dozen dishes that will start every day on the sunny side. A number of the recipes add excitement to familiar fare—you'll woo reluctant breakfast-skippers right back to the table. For brunch fests, too, we've included a host of fresh ideas, many that can helpfully be made the day before.

Chili Omelet

- 1 tablespoon butter or margarine
- 3 eggs, beaten
- 1 tablespoon milk
- ½ teaspoon salt
- Dash of pepper
- ¼ cup Armour Star Chili—No Beans*
- ¼ cup (1 oz.) shredded American cheese
- Chopped parsley

Melt butter or margarine in 6-inch fry pan over medium heat. Combine eggs, milk and seasonings; pour into fry pan. Reduce heat. As mixture sets, lift slightly with spatula to allow uncooked portion to flow underneath. When mixture is almost set, spoon chili over top; sprinkle with cheese. Fold in half. Garnish with parsley.

1 omelet

One can chili yields 8 omelets.

Scrambled Eggs Deluxe

- 1 2½-oz. jar Armour Star Sliced Dried Beef, rinsed, chopped
- 1 cup sliced mushrooms
- 4 tablespoons butter or margarine
- 6 eggs
- ⅓ cup milk
  - Dash of salt
  - Dash of pepper
- 1 tablespoon chopped parsley

In fry pan, cook dried beef and mushrooms in 3 tablespoons butter or margarine 10 minutes. Remove mixture; keep warm. Add remaining butter or margarine to pan. Combine eggs, milk, salt and pepper; pour into pan. Cook slowly, stirring until eggs are thickened but moist; remove to serving platter. Top with dried beef mixture; sprinkle with parsley.

4 servings

Microwave Instructions: *Cook dried beef, mushrooms and butter or margarine in 2-quart glass casserole, covered, on HIGH 3 minutes. Combine eggs and milk; pour into casserole. Stir. Cook, covered, on HIGH 6 to 8 minutes or until eggs are set, stirring occasionally. Stir in salt and pepper. Sprinkle with parsley.*

Sunrise Star

- ½ cup chopped onion
- ½ cup chopped green pepper
- 3 tablespoons butter or margarine
- 6 eggs
- ½ cup milk
- ½ teaspoon salt
- ¼ teaspoon pepper
- 8 white bread slices, toasted, buttered
- 4 slices Armour Star Cooked Ham

Heat oven to 350°. Cook onion and green pepper in butter or margarine 5 minutes or until tender. Spread evenly in 8-inch square baking dish. Combine eggs, milk, salt and pepper; pour over onion and green pepper. Bake at 350°, 15 minutes. Cut in quarters. For each serving, top one slice bread with one egg square, one slice ham and one slice bread.

4 servings

Microwave Instructions: *Melt butter or margarine in 8-inch square glass baking dish; stir in onion and green pepper. Cook on HIGH 2 to 3 minutes. Combine eggs, milk, salt and pepper; pour into dish. Cook, covered, on HIGH 6 to 7 minutes. Let stand 1 minute. Cut in quarters. For each serving, top one slice bread with one egg square, one slice ham and one slice bread.*

Salami Breakfast Eggs

- 1 4-oz. package Armour Star Hard Salami, chopped
- 6 eggs
- ⅓ cup milk
- ¼ teaspoon salt
- Dash of pepper
- 2 tablespoons butter or margarine
- 2 English muffins, split, toasted

Combine sausage, eggs, milk, salt and pepper. Melt butter or margarine; pour in sausage-egg mixture. Cook over low heat. When mixture starts to set, lift cooked portions with spatula; turn gently to cook all portions evenly. Serve on English muffins.

4 servings

Crunchy Breakfast Eggs

- ½ lb. Armour Star Polish Sausage, coarsely chopped
- ¼ cup chopped onion
- 2 tablespoons butter or margarine
- 6 eggs
- ⅓ cup milk
- ½ teaspoon salt
- ¼ teaspoon pepper
- ¼ cup crushed pretzels

Cook sausage and onion in butter or margarine until onion is tender, about 5 minutes. Combine eggs, milk, salt and pepper. Pour egg mixture over sausage and onion; cook over low heat. When mixture starts to set, lift cooked portions with spatula; turn gently to cook all portions evenly. Sprinkle with crushed pretzels.

4 servings

Microwave Instructions: Melt butter or margarine in 1½-quart glass casserole; stir in sausage and onion. Combine eggs and milk; pour into casserole. Cook, covered, on HIGH 8 minutes or until eggs are set, stirring occasionally. Stir in salt and pepper. Sprinkle with crushed pretzels.

Hot Dog Breakfast Hash

½ cup chopped green pepper
¼ cup chopped onion
½ cup butter or margarine
1 16-oz. package frozen hash brown potatoes
5 Armour Star Hot Dogs, sliced
1 teaspoon salt
¼ teaspoon pepper
4 eggs

In 10-inch fry pan, cook green pepper and onion in butter or margarine 5 minutes. Add potatoes; cook, covered, 15 minutes, stirring occasionally. Reduce heat. Add hot dogs, salt and pepper; mix lightly. Make 4 slight indentations in hash mixture and break eggs into them. Cook, covered, 7 to 10 minutes or until eggs are set.

4 servings

Muffin-Cup Breakfast

6 slices Armour Star Bacon, cooked until almost crisp
6 eggs
¼ cup half and half
1 tablespoon butter or margarine
Dash of salt
Dash of pepper

Heat oven to 350°. Cut a 1-inch piece from each bacon slice; place piece in bottom of each of 6 muffin cups. Wrap remaining bacon slices around sides of muffin cups. Break one egg in center of each. Top each with 2 teaspoons half and half, ½ teaspoon butter or margarine, salt and pepper. Bake at 350°, 15 to 20 minutes. Loosen edges with knife to remove.

6 servings

Mexicali Eggs

1 12-oz. can Armour Star Treet luncheon meat, sliced into 8 slices
2 tablespoons butter or margarine
1 cup finely chopped onion
8 eggs, slightly beaten
½ teaspoon salt
Dash of pepper
1 7-oz. can green chile salsa, heated

In fry pan, cook Treet on both sides until brown; remove from pan. Melt butter or margarine in fry pan; add onion. Cook until tender. Combine eggs and seasonings; pour into pan. Cook slowly, stirring occasionally until eggs are cooked. Spoon eggs over hot Treet slices. Pour salsa over top.

6 to 8 servings

Microwave Instructions: Melt butter or margarine in 2-quart glass casserole. Stir in onion; cook, covered, on HIGH 2 minutes. Combine eggs and seasonings; pour into casserole. Cook, covered, on HIGH 6 minutes, stirring halfway through cooking time. Arrange Treet slices in 12 × 8-inch glass baking dish; cook, covered, on HIGH 2 minutes. Spoon eggs over hot Treet slices. Pour salsa over top.

Eggs Benedict

4 slices (¼ inch thick) Armour Star Boneless Ham, heated
2 English muffins, split, toasted, buttered
4 eggs, poached
Hot hollandaise sauce

Place one slice ham on top of each muffin half; top with egg. Spoon hollandaise sauce over eggs.

2 servings

Denver Bacon Brunch

- 6 slices Armour Star Bacon
- 4 eggs, beaten
- ¼ cup mayonnaise
- 1 tablespoon instant chopped onion
- 2 teaspoons instant green bell pepper flakes

In fry pan, cook bacon until crisp; drain and crumble. Pour off all but 1 tablespoon bacon drippings. Combine eggs, mayonnaise, onion and bell pepper flakes; stir in bacon. Pour mixture into fry pan; cook on low heat, stirring occasionally until eggs are set.

2 servings

Microwave Instructions: *Cook bacon between layers of paper towel on HIGH 5½ to 6 minutes; crumble bacon. In 1-quart glass casserole, combine eggs, mayonnaise, onion and bell pepper flakes; stir in bacon. Cook, covered, on HIGH 2½ minutes, stirring halfway through cooking time. Stir. Let stand, covered, 2 minutes.*

Soufflé Lorraine

- 4 eggs, separated
- 1 16-oz. carton cottage cheese
- ½ cup grated Parmesan cheese
- ⅓ cup half and half
- 3 tablespoons flour
- 6 slices Armour Star Bacon, crisply cooked, crumbled
- ½ teaspoon salt
  Dash of pepper

Heat oven to 300°. Beat egg whites until stiff but not dry; set aside. Beat egg yolks until thick. Beat in cottage cheese, Parmesan cheese, half and half and flour; beat until almost smooth. Add bacon, salt and pepper; fold in egg whites. Pour into buttered 1½-quart soufflé dish or casserole. Bake at 300°, 1 hour.

6 servings

Quiche Lorraine

- 1½ cups milk
- 4 eggs, slightly beaten
- ½ teaspoon salt
  Dash of ground red pepper
- 2 cups (8 oz.) shredded Swiss cheese
- 2 tablespoons flour
- ½ lb. Armour Star Bacon, crisply cooked, crumbled
- 1 9-inch unbaked pastry shell
  Bacon Curls (below)
  Parsley sprigs

Heat oven to 350°. Combine milk, eggs and seasonings; mix well. Toss cheese with flour; add cheese mixture and bacon to egg mixture. Pour into pastry shell. Bake at 350°, 40 to 45 minutes. Garnish with Bacon Curls and parsley.

6 servings

BACON CURLS: Cook slices of Armour Star Bacon until almost crisp. Roll each slice around the tines of a fork to make a curl. Cook until crisp. Drain on absorbent paper.

Easy Bacon Preparation

PAN FRY: Place slices in cold fry pan. Cook over medium-low heat, 8 to 10 minutes on each side or until crisp, turning occasionally.

BROIL: Place slices on rack of broiler pan 3 inches from heat. Broil 2 to 3 minutes on each side or until crisp.

MICROWAVE: Place slices on double layer of paper towels or on microwave roasting rack in a shallow glass baking dish. Top with a layer of paper towel to prevent spattering. Cook on HIGH 1 minute per slice or until crisp.

Beef and Mushroom Quiche

- 1 9-inch frozen unbaked pastry shell, thawed
- 1 2½-oz. jar Armour Star Sliced Dried Beef, chopped
- ½ cup sliced mushrooms
- ⅓ cup chopped onion
- 3 tablespoons butter or margarine
- ¾ cup (3 oz.) shredded Swiss cheese
- 2 tablespoons flour
- 3 eggs, slightly beaten
- 1 cup milk
- ⅛ teaspoon ground red pepper

Heat oven to 400°. Bake pastry shell at 400°, 10 minutes; cool. Reduce oven temperature to 350°. In fry pan, cook dried beef, mushrooms and onion in butter or margarine on medium heat 10 minutes; spread mixture evenly in bottom of pastry shell. Toss cheese with flour; place on top of dried beef mixture. Combine remaining ingredients; pour over mixture in pastry shell. Bake at 350°, 40 minutes.

6 servings

Swiss Yodeler Pie

- 1¼ cups milk
- 4 eggs, slightly beaten
- ½ teaspoon salt
- Dash of ground red pepper
- 2 cups (8 oz.) shredded Swiss cheese
- 3 tablespoons flour
- 1 12-oz. can Armour Star Treet, chopped
- 2 9-inch frozen unbaked pastry shells, thawed

Heat oven to 350°. Combine milk, eggs and seasonings; mix well. Toss cheese with flour; add cheese mixture and Treet to egg mixture. Pour into pastry shells. Bake at 350°, 45 minutes or until set.

8 servings

Creamed Eggs and Beef

- 2 tablespoons butter or margarine
- 2 tablespoons flour
- ½ teaspoon salt
- Dash of white pepper
- 2 cups milk
- 1 8-oz. package cream cheese, softened
- 8 hard-cooked eggs, sliced
- 1 2½-oz. jar Armour Star Sliced Dried Beef, shredded
- 6 English muffins, split, toasted

In fry pan, melt butter or margarine on medium-low heat; stir in flour, salt and pepper. Gradually add milk, stirring until thickened. Reduce heat to low; fold in cream cheese, egg slices and dried beef. Heat through. Serve on English muffins.

6 servings

Corned Beef O'Brien

- ½ cup chopped onion
- ½ cup chopped green pepper
- 1 tablespoon butter or margarine
- 1 15-oz. can Armour Star Corned Beef Hash
- 1 cup (4 oz.) shredded Cheddar cheese

In fry pan, cook onion and green pepper in butter or margarine 5 minutes; add hash. Heat, stirring occasionally, until mixture is crisp and brown as desired. Sprinkle with cheese; cover pan. Heat 5 minutes.

2 servings

Microwave Instructions: *Melt butter or margarine in 1½-quart glass casserole. Stir in onion and green pepper; cook, covered, on HIGH 2 minutes. Stir in hash; cook, covered, on HIGH 4 minutes. Sprinkle with cheese; cook, uncovered, on HIGH 1 minute.*

Mock Monte Cristo Sandwich

- 8 white bread slices, crusts trimmed
- 1 2½-oz. jar Armour Star Sliced Dried Beef, rinsed
- 4 slices (4 oz.) Swiss cheese, cut in half
- 3 eggs, beaten
- 3 tablespoons milk
  Dash of salt
  Butter or margarine

Top one slice bread with 2 beef slices, cheese slice, 2 beef slices, cheese slice and one slice bread. Combine eggs, milk and salt; mix well. Dip each sandwich in egg mixture; grill in butter or margarine over medium heat until light brown on both sides. Cut each sandwich in quarters.

4 sandwiches

Breakfast Stroganoff

- 1 12-oz. package Armour Star Smokees, each cut in thirds
- 1 2½-oz. jar sliced mushrooms, drained
- ¼ cup chopped onion
- 2 tablespoons flour
- ¼ teaspoon salt
  Dash of pepper
- 1 teaspoon Armour Star Beef Flavor Instant Bouillon or 1 Armour Star Beef Flavor Bouillon cube dissolved in ¾ cup boiling water
- 1 cup dairy sour cream
- 4 English muffins, split, buttered, toasted

In fry pan, cook sausage, mushrooms and onion on medium heat 5 minutes. Stir in flour, salt and pepper; add bouillon. Heat thoroughly, stirring occasionally. Reduce heat to low; stir in sour cream. Heat 5 minutes. Serve on English muffins.

4 servings

Breakfast Steak Diane

- 4 Naturally Tender Beef Eye of Round Steaks, cut ¼ inch thick
- Salt
- Pepper
- ⅓ cup butter or margarine
- 1 tablespoon vegetable oil
- 1 tablespoon Worcestershire sauce
- 1 teaspoon dry mustard
- 1 tablespoon lemon juice
- 1 tablespoon chopped parsley
- 1 tablespoon chopped chives

Sprinkle steaks on each side with salt and pepper. In fry pan, cook steaks on medium-high heat in 1 tablespoon butter or margarine and oil 2 minutes on each side; remove steaks from fry pan. Melt remaining butter or margarine in fry pan; add Worcestershire sauce and dry mustard. Cook 2 minutes, stirring constantly. Return steaks to fry pan; cook 1 minute on each side. Remove steaks to hot platter. Add lemon juice, parsley and chives to fry pan; heat 1 minute, stirring constantly. Pour over steaks.

4 servings

Ham and Waffles Jubilee

- 6 slices (¼ inch thick) Golden Star Ham by Armour
- 2 tablespoons butter or margarine
- 1 21-oz. can cherry pie filling
- 6 frozen waffles, toasted

In fry pan, cook ham in butter or margarine. In saucepan, heat pie filling. Place one ham slice on each waffle; top with pie filling.

6 servings

Ham Griddle Cakes

    1 cup milk
    1 cup quick or old-fashioned oats
    2 tablespoons vegetable oil
    2 eggs
    ½ cup flour
    2 tablespoons sugar
    1 tablespoon baking powder
    1 cup diced Armour Star Boneless Ham
       Maple syrup, heated

Combine milk and oats; let stand 5 minutes. Add oil and eggs; mix well. Stir in flour, sugar and baking powder only until moistened; stir in ham. Cook on hot lightly greased griddle, using ¼ cup batter for each. Turn when top is bubbly and edges slightly dry. Serve with syrup.

4 servings

"Say Cheese" Rarebit

    ¼   cup butter or margarine
    ¼   cup flour
    1¾ cups milk
    1   cup (4 oz.) shredded Cheddar cheese
    1   2½-oz. jar Armour Star Sliced Dried Beef, rinsed, chopped
    ½   teaspoon Worcestershire sauce
        Dash of paprika
    4   white bread slices, toasted, cut in half

Melt butter or margarine; stir in flour. Slowly add milk, stirring until thickened. Reduce heat to low; stir in cheese. Add dried beef, Worcestershire sauce and paprika. Heat 5 minutes. Serve over toast.

4 servings

Hot Dog-Raisin Roll-Ups

- 1 7½-oz. package refrigerator biscuits
- 5 Armour Star Hot Dogs, cut in half crosswise
- ¼ cup brown sugar, packed
- 2 tablespoons raisins
- 2 tablespoons chopped walnuts
- ½ teaspoon cinnamon

Heat oven to 400°. Separate biscuits; flatten into 3x5-inch ovals. Top each with one hot dog piece. Combine brown sugar, raisins, walnuts and cinnamon; spoon 1 tablespoon of mixture over each hot dog piece. Seal edges of biscuit together; place seam side down on greased cookie sheet. Bake at 400°, 10 to 12 minutes or until brown.

10 buns

Orange-Nut Buns

- 1 7½-oz. package refrigerator biscuits
- ½ cup orange marmalade
- 2 tablespoons raisins
- 2 tablespoons chopped pecans
- 5 Armour Star Hot Dogs, cut in half crosswise

Heat oven to 400°. Separate biscuits; flatten into 3 × 5-inch ovals. Combine marmalade, raisins and pecans; spoon 1 tablespoon of mixture over each biscuit. Top with a hot dog piece. Seal edges of biscuit together; place seam side down on greased cookie sheet. Bake at 400°, 10 to 12 minutes or until brown.

10 buns

Appetizers & Snacks

It's easy entertaining . . . when Armour caters to you and your next party. These are irresistible hors d'oeuvres, and we've made sure the cook won't wilt in the kitchen while guests convene. And for anytime-eating, every recipe's a dandy snack: Stash some dips and spreads in the 'fridge for next-day nibbling. Bonus: When hungry kids line up, you'll be ready with healthful handouts.

Antipasto Appetizer Tray

1 10-oz. package frozen asparagus, cooked according to package directions
1 10-oz. package frozen cauliflower, partially cooked, cut into flowerets
1 6-oz. can pitted ripe olives, drained
1 cucumber, thinly sliced
1 cup cherry tomato halves
½ lb. mushrooms, sliced
1 8-oz. bottle Italian salad dressing
1 4-oz. package Armour Star Genoa Salami
1 4-oz. package Armour Star Tangy Beef Thuringer
1 6-oz. package sliced Provolone cheese, cut in quarters
  Lettuce leaves
  Carrot strips

Place vegetables in separate containers; pour dressing over vegetables. Cover; marinate in refrigerator overnight. Drain. Arrange vegetables, sausages and cheese on lettuce-covered platter. Garnish with carrot.

Ham-Filled Cream Puffs

- ½ cup water
- ¼ cup butter or margarine
- ½ cup flour
- ¼ teaspoon salt
- 2 eggs
- 2 cups chopped Armour Star Ham
- ¼ cup chopped sweet pickles
- ¼ cup chopped onion
- 2 tablespoons chopped pimiento
- ¼ cup mayonnaise

Heat oven to 400°. Bring water and butter or margarine to a boil. Add flour and salt; stir vigorously over low heat until mixture forms a ball. Remove from heat. Add eggs one at a time, beating well after each addition until mixture is smooth. Drop half-teaspoonfuls of batter onto ungreased cookie sheet. Bake at 400°, 30 minutes. Remove immediately from cookie sheet; cool. Combine remaining ingredients; mix well. Cut tops from cream puffs; fill bottoms with ham mixture. Replace tops.

48 appetizers

Chile-Ham Canapés

- 1 cup ground Armour's 1877 Ham
- 3 tablespoons mayonnaise
- 2 tablespoons chopped green chiles
- 1 tablespoon finely chopped onion
  Party rye bread slices
  Stuffed green olives, sliced

Combine ham, mayonnaise, chiles and onion; mix well. Chill. Spread on bread slices; top with olive slices.

1 cup

Party-Pleasers

- 1 French bread loaf
- 1 3-oz. can Armour Star Potted Meat Food Product
- 1 cup (4 oz.) shredded Cheddar cheese
- ½ cup butter or margarine, softened
- ¼ cup finely chopped onion

Slice bread into 12 slices. Combine potted meat, cheese, butter or margarine and onion; spread on bread slices. Broil 7 to 10 minutes or until brown.

12 appetizers

Individual Taco Pizzas

- 1 12½-oz. package Appian Way Pizza—Regular
- 1 15-oz can Armour Star Chili—No Beans
- ½ head lettuce, finely shredded
- ¼ cup finely chopped onion
- 1 cup chopped tomato
- 1 cup (4 oz.) shredded Cheddar cheese
- 1 avocado, peeled, sliced

Heat oven to 425°. Prepare pizza dough according to package directions; divide into 4 equal portions. Shape into 7-inch rounds on two greased cookie sheets. Spread each pizza with chili; cover with sauce. Bake at 425°, 18 to 20 minutes or until crusts are golden brown. Remove from oven; sprinkle each pizza with lettuce, onion, tomato, cheese and avocado.

4 servings

Southern Hospitality Rolls

    1 3-oz. package cream cheese, softened
    ¼ teaspoon Tabasco® sauce
    4 slices Armour Star Old Fashion Loaf, each cut in 3 strips
       Stuffed green olives, sliced

Combine cream cheese and Tabasco sauce. Spread 1 teaspoon mixture on each lunch meat strip; roll. Garnish with olive slice; chill.

12 appetizers

Savory Salami Wedges

    1 3-oz. package cream cheese, softened
    1 tablespoon chopped parsley
    1 teaspoon prepared mustard
    1 teaspoon prepared horseradish
    6 slices Armour Star Cooked Salami
       Parsley sprigs

Combine cream cheese, parsley, mustard and horseradish. Spread 5 slices of salami with cream cheese mixture, reserving 1 tablespoon; stack. Top with remaining slice of salami. Cut stack into eight wedges. Garnish each wedge with remaining cream cheese mixture and a tiny sprig of parsley; chill.

8 appetizers

Creamy Beef Roll-Ups

1 8-oz. package cream cheese, softened
2 tablespoons prepared horseradish or ¼ cup chopped green onions
1 2½-oz. jar Armour Star Sliced Dried Beef, rinsed

Combine cream cheese and horseradish or onions. Spread mixture on double dried beef slices; roll. Chill.

10 to 12 appetizers

Shamrock Pie

1 12½-oz. package Appian Way Pizza—Regular
1 15-oz. can Armour Star Corned Beef Hash
¼ cup chopped onion
1 2½-oz. jar sliced mushrooms, drained
1 2-oz. jar pimiento, cut in strips
1 cup green pepper strips

Heat oven to 425°. Prepare pizza dough according to package directions; spread on greased 10-inch pie plate. Combine hash, ½ can pizza sauce and onion; spread on dough. Top with remaining pizza sauce. Garnish with mushrooms, pimiento and green pepper. Bake at 425°, 18 to 20 minutes or until crust is golden brown.

3 to 4 servings

Rumaki

- 12 water chestnuts, cut in half
- 12 chicken livers, cut in half
- 12 slices Armour Star Bacon, cut in half
- 1 cup teriyaki sauce
- 1 cup brown sugar, packed

Wrap a piece of water chestnut and a piece of chicken liver in each piece of bacon; secure with wooden pick. Marinate in teriyaki sauce 4 hours; drain. Roll in brown sugar. Broil 3 to 4 inches from heat, 10 to 12 minutes, turning occasionally.

24 appetizers

South-of-the-Border Viennas

- 2 3$\frac{1}{8}$-oz. cans bean dip
- 28 round buttery crackers
- 1 cup (4 oz.) shredded Cheddar cheese
- 1 5-oz. can Armour Star Smoked Vienna Sausage, drained

Spread bean dip evenly on crackers; top with cheese. Cut sausages in half lengthwise, then in half crosswise; place one piece sausage on each cracker. Broil until cheese melts.

28 appetizers

Ham 'n Cheese Nut Log

  1 cup chopped Armour Star Boneless Ham
  1 cup (4 oz.) shredded Cheddar cheese
  1 3-oz. package cream cheese, softened
  1 tablespoon prepared horseradish
  ½ cup chopped pecans
    Party rye bread slices

Combine ham, cheeses and horseradish; blend thoroughly. Form into roll 1½ inches in diameter. Roll in chopped nuts. Chill. Serve with bread slices.

1 9-inch log

Tangy Spread

  2 3-oz. cans Armour Star Potted Meat Food Product
  1 8-oz. package cream cheese, softened
  1 tablespoon prepared horseradish
  1 tablespoon prepared mustard
    Bread or assorted crackers

Combine all ingredients; chill thoroughly. Serve on bread or crackers.

2 cups

Cottage Cheese-Beef Spread

  1 2½-oz. jar Armour Star Sliced Dried Beef, chopped
  1 16-oz. carton cottage cheese
  ¼ cup chopped green onions
  2 tablespoons dairy sour cream
    Assorted crackers

Combine all ingredients except crackers; chill. Serve on crackers.

2½ cups

Ham 'n Cheese Nut Log

Spinach-Beef Spread

- 1 10-oz. package frozen chopped spinach, thawed
- 1 8-oz. package cream cheese, softened
- 1 cup mayonnaise
- ½ cup chopped green onions
- 1 tablespoon dill weed
- 1 2½-oz. jar Armour Star Sliced Dried Beef, rinsed, chopped
  Assorted crackers

Combine spinach, cream cheese, mayonnaise, green onions and dill weed in container of electric blender; process on high speed 1 to 2 minutes or until smooth and creamy. Fold in dried beef; chill. Serve on crackers.

3 cups

Creamy Ham Spread

- 1 cup chopped Armour Star Boneless Ham
- 1 cup dairy sour cream
- 1 tablespoon prepared horseradish
  Party rye bread slices

Combine ham, sour cream and horseradish; chill. Serve with bread slices.

1½ cups

Beef 'n Cheese Nut Log

1 5-oz. jar Armour Star Sliced Dried Beef, rinsed, finely chopped
1 8-oz. package cream cheese, softened
1 cup (4 oz.) shredded Cheddar cheese
1 tablespoon prepared horseradish
½ cup chopped pecans
  Assorted crackers

Combine dried beef, cheeses and horseradish; blend thoroughly. Form into roll about 2 inches in diameter. Roll in chopped nuts. Chill. Serve with crackers.

1 8-inch log

Beefy Cheese Ball

1 2½-oz. jar Armour Star Sliced Dried Beef, rinsed, finely chopped
1 8-oz. package cream cheese, softened
¼ cup dairy sour cream
¼ cup grated Parmesan cheese
1 teaspoon prepared horseradish
  Assorted crackers

Combine ¼ cup dried beef, cream cheese, sour cream, Parmesan cheese and horseradish; blend thoroughly. Refrigerate mixture 15 minutes. Form into ball and roll in remaining dried beef. Chill thoroughly.. Serve on crackers.

Baked Beef Dip

 1 5-oz. jar Armour Star Sliced Dried Beef, rinsed, chopped
 2 8-oz. packages cream cheese, softened
 1 cup dairy sour cream
 ¼ cup milk
 4 teaspoons minced onion
 ½ teaspoon garlic salt
 1 cup chopped pecans, toasted
   Assorted crackers

Heat oven to 350°. Combine all ingredients except pecans and crackers; spoon into greased 12x8-inch baking dish. Top with pecans. Bake at 350°, 20 minutes. Cool 10 minutes; serve as a dip with crackers.

4 cups

Old English Potted Meat Spread

 1 5½-oz. can Armour Star Potted Meat Food Product
 1 5-oz. jar process cheese spread, sharp old English flavor
 3 tablespoons chopped sweet pickle
   Assorted crackers

Combine potted meat and cheese spread. Add pickle; chill. Serve on crackers.

1½ cups

Bacon-Mushroom Crowns

- 40 medium mushrooms
- ½ lb. Armour Star Bacon, crisply cooked, crumbled
- 1 cup (4 oz.) shredded Monterey Jack cheese
- ½ cup butter or margarine, softened
- ½ cup finely crushed corn chips
- 2 cloves garlic, crushed
- 2 tablespoons finely chopped onion
- 1 tablespoon dry red wine
- ½ teaspoon salt

Remove stems from cleaned mushrooms; chop stems. Combine stems with remaining ingredients. Fill mushroom caps; place on baking sheet stuffing side up. Broil 5 to 7 minutes or until light brown and bubbly.

40 appetizers

Microwave Instructions: *Remove stems from cleaned mushrooms; chop stems. Combine stems with remaining ingredients. Fill mushroom caps; place half of mushrooms in glass baking dish stuffing side up. Cook on HIGH, 3 to 4 minutes. Repeat with remaining mushrooms.*

Mushrooms Elegant

- 2 cups chopped Golden Star Ham by Armour
- ½ cup (2 oz.) grated Parmesan cheese
- ½ cup mayonnaise
- 36 large mushrooms (about 1 lb.)

Combine ham, cheese and mayonnaise. Remove stems from mushrooms; fill caps with ham mixture. Place on broiler pan; broil 5 to 7 minutes or until filling is golden brown.

36 appetizers

Glazed Hot Dog Dunkers

- 1 cup grape jelly
- ½ cup lemon juice
- 3 tablespoons cornstarch
- ¼ teaspoon ground cinnamon
- 1 lb. Armour Star Hot Dogs, cut in ½-inch pieces
- 1 8-oz. can water chestnuts, drained
- 1 medium green pepper, cut into chunks

In large fry pan, combine jelly, lemon juice, cornstarch and cinnamon. Heat, stirring constantly, until glaze thickens and jelly melts. Add hot dogs, water chestnuts and green pepper, stirring to coat pieces; heat through. Serve with wooden picks.

64 appetizers

Chili-Onion Cups

- 12 small onions
- 1 15½-oz. can Armour Star Chili with Beans
- ½ cup crushed saltine crackers
- 2 tablespoons water
- 4 slices (4 oz.) Swiss cheese, cut in 2-inch strips
- 2 tablespoons chopped parsley

Heat oven to 350°. Remove ends and outer skins from onions. Cook in boiling salted water 20 minutes or until tender; drain. Remove centers of onions. Combine chili and crackers; spoon mixture into onions. Place in 8-inch square baking dish; add water. Bake, covered, at 350°, 25 minutes. Top with cheese strips and parsley. Bake, uncovered, 5 minutes or until cheese melts.

12 appetizers

Crispy Barbecue Bites

- 1 cup pancake mix
- ½ cup milk
- 1 egg
- 1 tablespoon vegetable oil
- 2 5-oz. cans Armour Star Vienna Sausage in Barbecue Sauce, drained, reserving sauce
- Vegetable oil, heated
- 1 cup dairy sour cream
- Dash of Tabasco sauce

Combine pancake mix, milk, egg and vegetable oil; mix well. Cut sausages in half crosswise; coat with pancake batter. Fry in ¾ inch of hot oil until golden brown on both sides. Drain. Combine reserved barbecue sauce, sour cream and Tabasco sauce. Serve as a dip for sausage pieces.

28 appetizers

Tasty 'Tater Tidbits

- 6 slices Armour Star Bologna, cut in thirds
- 18 frozen shredded potato rounds, thawed
- ¼ cup barbecue sauce

Heat oven to 400°. Wrap each bologna piece around each potato round. Thread bologna-potato rounds on skewers; brush with barbecue sauce. Bake at 400°, 10 minutes.

18 appetizers

Meaty Deviled Eggs

- 6 hard-cooked eggs, cut in halves
- 1 3-oz. can Armour Star Potted Meat Food Product
- 2 tablespoons sweet pickle relish
- 1 tablespoon mayonnaise
- ½ teaspoon vinegar
- ½ teaspoon prepared mustard
- ½ teaspoon paprika
- ¼ teaspoon onion powder
- ⅛ teaspoon garlic powder
- Parsley sprigs

Remove yolks from eggs. Mash yolks; blend in remaining ingredients except parsley. Fill egg halves. Chill thoroughly. Garnish with parsley.

12 servings

Hot Chili-Cheese Dip

- 1 15-oz. can Armour Star Chili—No Beans
- 1 4-oz. can chopped green chiles
- 1 lb. process American cheese, shredded
- 1 tablespoon Worcestershire sauce
- Corn chips

Combine all ingredients, except chips; heat, stirring occasionally, over low heat until cheese melts. Serve as a dip with chips.

4 cups

Microwave Instructions: *Combine all ingredients, except chips, in 1½-quart glass casserole. Cook, covered, on HIGH 6 minutes, stirring occasionally. Serve as a dip with chips.*

Center: Meaty Deviled Eggs
Top: Hot Chili-Cheese Dip
Bottom: Cheesy Meat Spread, Creamy Beef Dip

Cheesy Meat Spread

1 3-oz. can Armour Star Potted Meat Food Product
1 7½-oz. container pimiento cheese spread
½ cup mayonnaise
2 tablespoons chopped parsley
1 tablespoon minced onion
   Assorted crackers

Combine all ingredients; beat at medium speed of electric mixer until smooth. Chill thoroughly. Serve on crackers.

1¼ cups

Creamy Beef Dip

1 2½-oz. jar Armour Star Sliced Dried Beef, rinsed, chopped
1 8-oz. package cream cheese, softened
¼ cup milk
1 teaspoon dill weed
½ teaspoon prepared horseradish
   Assorted fresh vegetables

Combine dried beef, cream cheese, milk, dill weed and horseradish; chill. Serve as a dip with vegetables.

1½ cups

Festive Ham Apple-tizers

- ½ cup brown sugar, packed
- 1 tablespoon cornstarch
- ¼ teaspoon ground cloves
- Dash of ground ginger
- ½ cup lemon juice
- 1 lb. Armour Star Boneless Ham, cut into ¾-inch cubes
- 2 large apples, cut into chunks
- 1 cup small mushrooms, quartered

In large skillet, combine brown sugar, cornstarch, cloves and ginger; add lemon juice. Heat, stirring constantly until thickened. Add ham, apples and mushrooms, stirring to coat pieces; heat through. Serve with wooden picks.

6 cups

Spicy Cantonese Appetizers

- 1 10-oz. jar currant jelly
- ½ cup prepared mustard
- 6 Armour Star Dinner Franks, cut in ½-inch pieces

In saucepan, heat jelly and mustard 5 minutes. Add franks; continue heating 10 minutes. Serve with wooden picks.

60 appetizers

Glazed Ham Bits

1 lb. Armour Star Boneless Ham, cut in 1-inch cubes
1 10-oz. jar sweet and sour sauce

Brush ham with sweet and sour sauce. Broil 3 to 5 minutes. Serve with wooden picks.

36 appetizers

Sausage Bits with Mustard Dip

1 lb. Armour Star Smoked Sausage
1 12-oz. can beer
1 tablespoon prepared mustard
2 tablespoons dry mustard
2 tablespoons hot water
2 tablespoons dairy sour cream
1 tablespoon vinegar
¼ teaspoon ginger

Simmer sausage in beer and prepared mustard for 15 minutes; drain. Cut sausage in 1-inch pieces. Combine dry mustard, water, sour cream, vinegar and ginger. Serve as a dip with sausage.

24 appetizers

Microwave Instructions: *Place sausage, beer and prepared mustard in 2-quart glass casserole. Cook, covered, on HIGH 7 to 9 minutes; drain. Cut sausage in 1-inch pieces. Combine dry mustard, water, sour cream, vinegar and ginger. Serve as dip with sausage.*

Ham Scallops with Mustard Dip

- ¾ cup dry bread crumbs
- ½ cup flour
- ¼ teaspoon ground cloves
- 1 lb. Armour Star Ham, cut in ¾-inch cubes
- 1 cup buttermilk
  Vegetable oil
- 1 cup dairy sour cream
- 2 teaspoons prepared mustard

Mix crumbs, flour and cloves. Dip ham cubes in buttermilk; roll in crumb mixture. Heat oil to 375°. Fry coated ham cubes 3 to 5 minutes or until golden brown. Combine sour cream and mustard. Serve as a dip with ham scallops.

30 appetizers

Deviled Ham Dip

- 1 cup ground Armour's 1877 Ham
- 3 tablespoons mayonnaise
- 2 tablespoons chili sauce
- 1 tablespoon prepared mustard
- ½ teaspoon chili powder
- ½ teaspoon brown sugar, packed
  Assorted crackers

Combine all ingredients except crackers; mix well. Chill. Serve with crackers.

1¼ cups

Lunches

A meal-in-a-bowl or a meal-in-a-bun? Lucky the lunchmaker who leans on Armour . . . for frankly fast sandwiches hot 'n cold, for filling soups and hearty salads, for invigorating platters that revive energy for the rest of the day. Here are simple-to-splendid creations for any kind of midday meal. Many are seasoned travelers: Tuck them away in brown bags and lunch boxes; fill up a picnic basket for summer safaris. For every kind of lunch you can imagine, you'll find everything here . . . from everything Armour.

Hawaiian Salad

1 cup Armour Star Spiced Luncheon Meat, cut in julienne strips
2 cups shredded cabbage
1 cup shredded lettuce
1 cup chopped celery
1 20-oz. can pineapple chunks, drained
¼ cup chopped green pepper
1 tablespoon vinegar
1 teaspoon prepared horseradish

Combine all ingredients; toss lightly. Chill thoroughly.

4 to 6 servings

Turkey-Fruit Toss

- 2 cups cubed cooked Armour Golden Star Young Turkey
- 3 bananas, sliced
- ½ cup chopped celery
- ½ cup chopped pecans
- ½ cup mayonnaise
- 2 tablespoons finely chopped onion
- 2 teaspoons lemon juice
- 1 teaspoon salt
- ¼ teaspoon dill weed
- Dash of pepper
- Lettuce cups
- Jellied cranberry sauce

In large bowl, combine all ingredients except lettuce and cranberry sauce. Cover; chill until ready to serve. Spoon mixture into lettuce cups; top each serving with cranberry sauce.

4 servings

Apple-Turkey Toss

- 2 cups cubed cooked Armour Golden Star Boneless Young Turkey
- 2 cups chopped apples
- 1 cup sliced celery
- ⅔ cup mayonnaise
- ¼ cup slivered almonds
- 2 tablespoons lemon juice
- ½ teaspoon basil leaves, crushed
- ½ teaspoon ground sage
- ½ teaspoon salt
- Lettuce cups
- 2 hard-cooked eggs, sliced

Combine all ingredients except eggs and lettuce; toss lightly. Spoon into lettuce cups. Top with eggs.

6 servings

Tempting Turkey Salad

- 4 cups chopped cooked Armour Golden Star Young Turkey
- 1 cup chopped celery
- 1 cup chopped green pepper
- 2 teaspoons grated onion
- ⅔ cup mayonnaise
- ¼ cup half and half
- 2 tablespoons vinegar
- 1 teaspoon salt
- Dash of pepper
- Lettuce cups

Combine turkey, celery, green pepper and onion. Blend together mayonnaise, half and half, vinegar, salt and pepper. Toss with turkey mixture; chill. Serve in lettuce cups.

6 servings

Curried Turkey-Fruit Salad

- ¾ cup mayonnaise
- 2 tablespoons lemon juice
- ½ teaspoon curry powder
- ½ teaspoon salt
- 2 cups chopped cooked Armour Golden Star Young Turkey
- 1 13½-oz. can pineapple tidbits, drained
- 1 11-oz. can mandarin oranges, drained
- ½ cup chopped apple
- ½ cup chopped pecans
- 12 maraschino cherries, quartered
- Lettuce cups

Combine mayonnaise, lemon juice, curry and salt. Add remaining ingredients except lettuce; toss lightly. Chill. Serve in lettuce cups.

6 servings

Ham Confetti Mousse

- 2 envelopes unflavored gelatin
- 2 cups milk
- ¼ cup butter or margarine
- 3 tablespoons flour
- 1 cup mayonnaise
- ½ teaspoon salt
- ½ teaspoon prepared mustard
- 3 cups finely chopped Armour Star Boneless Ham
- 1 cup finely chopped celery
- ½ cup finely chopped green pepper
- ¼ cup grated onion
- Lettuce leaves

Dissolve gelatin in ½ cup milk. Melt butter or margarine in saucepan; blend in flour. Gradually add remaining milk; cook, stirring constantly until thickened. Stir in mayonnaise, salt, mustard and gelatin. Add ham, celery, green pepper and onion. Pour into lightly greased 1-quart mold. Chill until set or overnight. Unmold on lettuce-lined platter.

6 to 8 servings

Ham-Orange Salad

- 2 cups cubed Armour's 1877 Ham
- 1 11-oz. can mandarin oranges, drained
- 1 cup thinly sliced celery
- ½ cup chopped walnuts
- ⅓ cup chopped green onions
- Creamy garlic salad dressing

Combine all ingredients except salad dressing. Chill. Just before serving, toss with salad dressing.

4 servings

Ham-Macaroni Salad

- 2 cups Armour Star Ham, cut in julienne strips
- 3 cups cooked shell macaroni
- 1 cup chopped celery
- 1 cup cherry tomato halves
- 1 cup whole pitted ripe olives
- ½ cup Italian salad dressing

Combine all ingredients; toss lightly. Chill.

8 servings

Vegetable-Patch Salad

- 2 5-oz. cans Armour Star Vienna Sausage in Beef Stock, drained, sliced
- 2 cups cooked elbow macaroni
- 1 17¼-oz. jar marinated garbanzo beans, drained
- 1 15¼-oz. can kidney beans, drained
- 2 tomatoes, cut up
- ½ cup Italian salad dressing
- ½ cup chopped green pepper
- ¼ cup chopped green onions
- ½ teaspoon salt

Combine all ingredients; mix well. Chill several hours.

8 to 10 servings

Ham Waldorf Salad

- 2 medium apples, quartered, cored, cubed
- 1 tablespoon lemon juice
- 1 cup cubed Armour Star Chopped Ham
- ¼ cup sliced celery
- ¼ cup mayonnaise
- 2 tablespoons chopped walnuts

In large bowl, toss apples with lemon juice. Add remaining ingredients; mix well. Chill.

3 to 4 servings

Swiss Salami Salad

- 1 4-oz. package Armour Star Hard Salami, sliced in thin strips
- 1 cup (4 oz.) shredded Swiss cheese
- ¼ cup chopped green pepper
- ¼ cup chopped celery
- 2 tablespoons chopped green onions
- ⅓ cup mayonnaise
- 1 cup croutons
  Lettuce cups
  Grated Parmesan cheese

Combine salami, Swiss cheese, green pepper, celery, onions and mayonnaise; chill. Just before serving, add croutons; toss lightly. Serve in lettuce cups; sprinkle with Parmesan cheese.

4 servings

Confetti Cottage Cheese

1 4-oz. package Armour Star Hard Salami, finely chopped
2 cups cottage cheese
⅓ cup chopped green onions
2 tablespoons dairy sour cream
   Lettuce cups

Combine all ingredients except lettuce. Serve in lettuce cups.

4 servings

Smackaroni Salad

1 4-oz. package Armour Star Hard Salami, cut in julienne strips
2 **cups cooked shell macaroni**
1 cup chopped celery
1 cup cherry tomato halves
1 cup whole pitted ripe olives
½ cup finely chopped green pepper
¼ cup finely chopped green onions
½ cup Italian salad dressing
1 teaspoon salt

Combine all ingredients; toss lightly. Chill.

6 servings

Irish Mac Salad

- 1 12-oz. can Armour Star Corned Beef, shredded
- 2 cups cooked elbow macaroni
- 1 cup dairy sour cream
- ¼ cup chopped green pepper
- ¼ cup chopped celery
- 2 tablespoons chopped onion
- 1 teaspoon salt
- 1 teaspoon prepared mustard
- ¼ teaspoon pepper
-   Lettuce cups

Combine all ingredients except lettuce cups; chill thoroughly. Serve in lettuce cups.

6 servings

Country Vegetable Sandwich

- 2 tablespoons catsup
- 2 tablespoons mayonnaise
- 1 tablespoon grated onion
- 8 whole wheat bread slices, toasted
-   Lettuce leaves
-   Cucumber slices
-   Radish slices
- 4 slices Armour Star Pickle Loaf

Combine catsup, mayonnaise and onion; spread mixture on bread slices. For each sandwich top one slice bread with lettuce, cucumber, radish, one slice lunch meat and one slice bread.

4 sandwiches

Skyscraper

- 3 thin white bread slices
  Mayonnaise
- 1 slice Armour Star Pickle Loaf
  Lettuce leaves
- 2 slices Armour Star Bologna
  Tomato slices

Spread each slice bread with mayonnaise. Cover first slice bread with pickle loaf, lettuce, second slice bread, one slice bologna, tomato slices, second slice bologna and third slice bread.

1 sandwich

Devilish Meat and Egg Sandwich

- 5 hard-cooked eggs
- 2 3-oz. cans Armour Star Potted Meat Food Product
- ⅓ cup mayonnaise
- 2 tablespoons sweet pickle relish
- 1 tablespoon minced onion
- 12 white bread slices
  Lettuce

Mash eggs; mix with potted meat food product, mayonnaise, pickle relish and onion; chill, if desired. Spread mixture on 6 bread slices; top with lettuce and remaining bread slices.

6 sandwiches

Gondolier's Sandwich

- 4 French bread rolls, split
  Shredded lettuce
- 1 4-oz. package Armour Star Genoa Salami
- 1 4-oz. package Armour Star Sweet Peperoni
- 4 slices Provolone cheese, cut in half
  Tomato slices
- 2 hard-cooked eggs, sliced
  Sliced pitted ripe olives
  Italian salad dressing

For each sandwich, cover bottom half of roll with lettuce, salami, peperoni, cheese, tomato, egg slices, olives, salad dressing and top of roll.

4 sandwiches

Crunchy Cranberry Sandwich

- ⅓ cup finely chopped apple
- ⅓ cup chopped cranberries
- ⅓ cup chopped salted almonds
- 2 tablespoons finely chopped celery
- 2 tablespoons sugar
- ¼ cup mayonnaise
- 8 whole wheat bread slices
- 4 slices Armour Star Bologna

Combine apple, cranberries, almonds, celery, sugar and 2 tablespoons mayonnaise. Spread mixture on 4 slices bread; top each with one slice bologna. Spread remaining bread with remaining mayonnaise and top sandwiches.

4 sandwiches

Easy-Time Sandwich

- 2 white bread slices
  Salad dressing
  Prepared mustard
- 2 slices Armour Star Treet luncheon meat
- 1 slice process American cheese
  Sweet pickle relish, drained

Spread bread with salad dressing and mustard. Top one slice bread with one slice Treet, cheese, relish, remaining slice Treet and bread.

1 sandwich

Leftover-Magic Turkey Stack

- 2 3-oz. packages cream cheese, softened
- ¼ cup (1 oz.) blue cheese, crumbled
- ⅓ cup chopped stuffed green olives
- 1 teaspoon grated onion
- 12 whole wheat bread slices
  Mayonnaise
- 6 slices cooked Armour Golden Star Boneless Young Turkey
- 1½ cups leftover poultry stuffing
- 1 16-oz. can whole berry cranberry sauce, chilled, sliced
  Lettuce leaves

Combine cream cheese, blue cheese, olives and onion. Spread 6 bread slices with mayonnaise; stack each with turkey slice, ¼ cup stuffing, cranberry sauce and lettuce. Spread cheese mixture on each remaining bread slice; invert on top of lettuce. Secure with picks and cut.

6 sandwiches

Bacon-Avocado-Tomato Sandwich

 1 ripe avocado, peeled, mashed
¼ cup mayonnaise
 1 teaspoon lemon juice
   Dash of salt
½ cup chopped tomatoes
12 slices Armour Star Bacon, crisply cooked
 4 whole wheat bread slices

Combine avocado, mayonnaise, lemon juice and salt; mix well. Stir in tomatoes. Spread ¼ of mixture on each bread slice; top with 3 slices bacon.

4 sandwiches

Chef's Sandwich

4 French bread rolls, split, buttered
  Lettuce leaves
2 hard-cooked eggs, sliced
4 slices Armour Star Cooked Ham
4 slices Armour Star Cooked Salami
2 slices process American cheese, cut in julienne strips
2 slices Swiss cheese, cut in julienne strips
  French salad dressing

For each sandwich, cover bottom half of roll with lettuce, egg slices, one slice ham, one slice salami, cheese strips, 1 tablespoon salad dressing and top of roll.

4 sandwiches

Deli Sandwich

    4 white bread slices
       Butter or margarine, softened
       Lettuce leaves
       Tomato slices
    4 slices process American cheese
    2 slices Armour Star Pimento Loaf
    2 slices Armour Star Spiced Luncheon Meat
       Coleslaw

Spread bread with butter or margarine; cover 2 slices of bread with lettuce, tomato, cheese, lunch meat and coleslaw. Top with remaining slices of bread.

2 sandwiches

The Works

    1 individual pita bread, split in half crosswise
       Mayonnaise
    1 slice Armour Star Bologna
       Alfalfa sprouts
    1 slice Armour Star Cooked Salami
       Tomato slices

Spread insides of pita bread with mayonnaise. Cover with bologna, alfalfa sprouts, salami, tomato slices and top of bread.

1 sandwich

Orange Blossom Sandwich

- 2 whole wheat bread slices, toasted, buttered
- 2 slices Armour Star Cooked Salami
- 1 orange, peeled, thinly sliced crosswise
- 2 slices Monterey Jack cheese
- 2 whole strawberries

For each sandwich, cover one slice bread with one slice salami, orange slices and one slice cheese. Broil 5 minutes or until cheese is melted. Garnish with strawberry.

2 sandwiches

Open-Face Summer Sandwich

- 8 slices rye bread
- 16 thin slices Armour Star Spiced Luncheon Meat
- 1 16-oz. can sauerkraut, drained
  Creamy Horseradish Sauce (below)

On each slice of rye bread arrange spiced luncheon meat slices, sauerkraut and sauce. Broil 4 to 5 minutes or until sauce is light brown and bubbly.

8 sandwiches

CREAMY HORSERADISH SAUCE: Combine 1 cup mayonnaise, ½ cup dairy sour cream, 2 tablespoons prepared horseradish, ½ teaspoon dry mustard; mix well. Makes 1½ cups sauce.

Brown-Bagger Basic

- 2 whole wheat bread slices
  Butter or margarine, softened
  Prepared mustard
- 2 slices Armour Star Cooked Salami
- 1 slice Monterey Jack cheese

Spread bread with butter or margarine and mustard. Top first slice of bread with salami, cheese and second slice of bread.

1 sandwich

Cheesy Open-Face Sandwich

- ½ cup thinly sliced onion
- 3 tablespoons butter or margarine
- 3 tablespoons flour
- ½ teaspoon salt
- ½ teaspoon thyme
  Dash of pepper
- 2 teaspoons Armour Star Beef Flavor Instant Bouillon or 2 Armour Star Beef Flavor Bouillon cubes dissolved in ½ cup boiling water
- 1¼ cups milk
- 1 8-oz. package medium Cheddar cheese, shredded
- 8 tomato slices
- 1 10-oz. package frozen asparagus spears, cooked according to package directions
- 4 white bread slices, toasted

Heat oven to 325°. Cook onion in butter or margarine 5 minutes or until tender; stir in flour and seasonings. Add bouillon and milk. Heat, stirring constantly until thickened. Stir in 1½ cups cheese. In a 13 × 9-inch baking dish, layer tomato slices and asparagus; cover with sauce. Sprinkle evenly with remaining cheese. Bake at 325°, 15 minutes. Serve over toast.

4 servings

Peanut Butter-Bologna Grill

  4 white bread slices
      Peanut butter
  4 slices Armour Star Bologna
      Butter or margarine

Spread bread slices with peanut butter; top two slices of bread with two slices bologna and second slice of bread. Spread bread with butter or margarine; grill on both sides until light brown.

2 sandwiches

Picadilly Sandwich

  1 12-oz. can Armour Star Treet luncheon meat, chopped
  ½ cup drained sauerkraut
  ¼ cup chopped dill pickles
  ¼ cup mayonnaise
  1 tablespoon prepared mustard
16 rye bread slices
  8 slices (8 oz.) process Swiss cheese
      Butter or margarine

Combine Treet, sauerkraut, pickles, mayonnaise and mustard. For each sandwich, spread slice of bread with mixture; cover with slice of cheese and second slice of bread. Spread outside of sandwich with butter or margarine. Grill on both sides until golden brown.

8 sandwiches

Microwave Instructions: *Prepare sandwich as directed above. Preheat microwave browning skillet on HIGH 3 minutes. Place sandwich on skillet; cook 45 seconds. Turn sandwich; cook 1 minute or until golden brown.*

Bacon Broil Sandwich

- 8 slices Armour Star Bacon, partially cooked, cut in 1-inch pieces
- 1 cup (4 oz.) shredded Cheddar cheese
- ½ cup mayonnaise
- ½ cup chopped celery
- ¼ cup chopped green pepper
- 2 tablespoons chopped onion
- 3 hamburger buns, split, toasted

Combine bacon, cheese, mayonnaise and vegetables. Place ¼ cup of mixture on each bun half. Broil 5 to 6 inches from heat, 4 to 5 minutes or until mixture is hot and bubbly.

6 sandwiches

Bacon Cheesewich

- 8 slices Armour Star Bacon
- ½ cup thinly sliced onion
- ½ cup thinly sliced green pepper rings
- 4 white bread slices, toasted
- Mayonnaise
- Catsup
- 4 slices process American cheese

Crisply cook bacon; drain, reserving 2 tablespoons drippings. Cook onion and green pepper in drippings until tender, about 5 minutes. Spread toast with mayonnaise and catsup; top with onion, green pepper and cheese. Broil 5 minutes or until cheese is melted. Crisscross bacon over top.

4 sandwiches

Corned Beef Meltaways

 6 onion rolls, split
   Prepared horseradish mustard
 1 lb. cooked sliced Armour Star Corned Beef, Brisket or Round
 6 slices Provolone cheese

Heat oven to 400°. For each sandwich, spread bottom half of onion roll with mustard; top with corned beef slices, cheese slice and top of roll. Wrap in aluminum foil. Bake at 400°, 20 minutes.

6 sandwiches

Reuben Melt

 1 12-oz. can Armour Star Corned Beef
 ½ cup mayonnaise
 8 rye bread slices, toasted on one side
 1 16-oz. can sauerkraut, drained
 8 slices (8 oz.) process Swiss cheese

Combine corned beef and mayonnaise; spread on untoasted sides of bread. Top with sauerkraut and cheese. Broil 3 minutes or until cheese melts.

8 sandwiches

Golden Salami Grill

- 2 white bread slices
  Prepared mustard
- 2 slices Armour Star Cooked Salami
- 1 slice process American cheese
- 2 tomato slices
- 1 onion slice, separated into rings
  Butter or margarine

Spread bread with mustard. Top one slice bread with salami, cheese, tomato, onion and bread. Spread outside of sandwich with butter or margarine; grill until light brown.

1 sandwich

Kraut-Wurst Sandwich

- 1 lb. Armour Star Kulbassy, split lengthwise
- 1 16-oz. can sauerkraut, drained
- 4 French bread rolls, split lengthwise, toasted
  Mayonnaise
  Prepared horseradish mustard

Brown sausage in fry pan. Add sauerkraut; cover and heat 15 minutes. For each sandwich, spread bottom of roll with mayonnaise and top of roll with horseradish mustard. Top bottom of roll with sausage, sauerkraut and top of roll.

4 sandwiches

Chili Dogs

8 Armour Star Hot Dogs, heated
8 frankfurter buns, heated
1 15-oz. can Armour Star Chili—No Beans, heated
Shredded Cheddar cheese
Chopped onion

Place each hot dog in a bun; top with chili, cheese and onion.

8 sandwiches

Joes' Dogs

1 15½-oz. can Armour Star Sloppy Joes
8 Armour Star Hot Dogs, heated
8 frankfurter buns, heated
Shredded Cheddar cheese
Chopped onion

In saucepan, heat sloppy Joes. Place each hot dog in a bun; top with sloppy Joes, cheese and onion.

8 sandwiches

Coney Island Hot Dogs

8 Armour Star Hot Dogs, heated
8 frankfurter buns, heated
Prepared mustard
Sweet pickle relish
Finely chopped onion

Place each hot dog in a bun. Top with mustard, relish and onion.

8 sandwiches

Chili Dogs

Deviled Dogs

- 1 cup (4 oz.) shredded process American cheese
- ⅓ cup sweet pickle relish, drained
- 3 tablespoons mayonnaise
- 1 tablespoon chili sauce
- 1 teaspoon prepared mustard
- 8 Armour Star Hot Dogs, split lengthwise
- 8 frankfurter buns

Combine cheese, pickle relish, mayonnaise, chili sauce and mustard; stuff 2 tablespoons mixture into each hot dog. Broil 5 to 6 inches from heat 7 to 9 minutes or until cheese is slightly melted. Place each hot dog in a bun.

8 sandwiches

Campfire Picnic Buns

- 1 6-oz. package Armour Star Bologna
- 1 cup (4 oz.) shredded Cheddar cheese
- 3 tablespoons mayonnaise
- 2 tablespoons sweet pickle relish, drained
- 1½ teaspoons prepared mustard
- 1 teaspoon grated onion
- 6 frankfurter buns, split

Heat oven to 375°. Slice bologna in very thin strips. Add cheese, mayonnaise, relish, mustard and onion; mix well. Fill buns with mixture; wrap each bun in foil. Bake at 375°, 20 minutes or place on grill over medium heat until cheese melts and buns are hot.

6 sandwiches

Sailor's Stew

3 French bread rolls, cut in half lengthwise
1 24-oz. can Armour Star Beef Stew, heated
1 cup (4 oz.) shredded Cheddar cheese

Hollow out roll halves; broil until light brown. Fill each roll with beef stew, using slotted spoon. Sprinkle with cheese; broil until cheese melts.

6 servings

Pizza Loaf

1 lb. Naturally Tender Ground Beef
1 6-oz. can tomato paste
½ cup finely chopped onion
½ cup grated Parmesan cheese
¼ cup chopped pitted ripe olives
1 teaspoon garlic salt
1 teaspoon salt
½ teaspoon oregano
1 loaf unsliced Italian bread, cut in half lengthwise
2 tomatoes, sliced
2 cups (8 oz.) shredded Mozzarella cheese

Combine ground beef, tomato paste, onion, Parmesan cheese, olives, garlic salt, salt and oregano; mix well. Spread mixture on bread halves; broil 5 inches from heat, 12 to 15 minutes or until light brown. Top with tomatoes and Mozzarella cheese. Broil 5 minutes or until cheese melts.

6 to 8 servings

Garden-Variety Pizza

- 1 12½-oz. package Appian Way Pizza—Regular
- ¼ cup chopped onion
- ¼ cup chopped green pepper
- ¼ cup sliced pitted ripe olives
- 1 2½-oz. jar sliced mushrooms, drained
- 1 12-oz. can Armour Star Treet, chopped
- 1 cup (4 oz.) shredded Mozzarella cheese

Heat oven to 425°. Prepare pizza dough according to package directions; cover with sauce. Sprinkle with remaining ingredients. Bake at 425°, 18 to 20 minutes or until crust is golden brown.

3 to 4 servings

Peperoni Pizza

- 1 12½-oz. package Appian Way Pizza—Regular
- 1 4-oz. package Armour Star Caserta Brand Peperoni
- 1 2½-oz. jar sliced mushrooms, drained
- ¼ cup sliced pitted ripe olives
- ¼ cup chopped green pepper
- ¼ cup chopped onion
- 1 cup (4 oz.) shredded Mozzarella cheese

Heat oven to 425°. Prepare pizza dough according to package directions; cover with sauce. Sprinkle with remaining ingredients. Bake at 425°, 18 to 20 minutes or until crust is golden brown.

3 to 4 servings

Hash Patties

- 1 15-oz. can Armour Star Corned Beef Hash
- 1 cup soft bread crumbs
- 1 egg, slightly beaten
- 3 tablespoons finely chopped green onions
  Dash of pepper
- 2 tablespoons butter or margarine
- ½ cup dairy sour cream

Combine hash, bread crumbs, egg, 1 tablespoon onions and pepper; mix until well blended. Shape into 6 patties. Cook patties in butter or margarine over medium-low heat 10 minutes or until brown on both sides; turn only once. Top patties with sour cream and remaining onions.

3 servings

Sloppy Joes Olé

- 1 15½-oz. can Armour Star Sloppy Joes
- ½ cup chopped onion
- ½ cup chopped green pepper
- 1 cup (4 oz.) shredded Cheddar cheese
- ¼ cup sliced pitted ripe olives
  Corn bread

Combine sloppy Joes, onion and green pepper. Simmer, covered, 15 minutes. Stir in cheese and olives. Serve over corn bread.

3 servings

Microwave Instructions: *Combine sloppy Joes, onion and green pepper in 1-quart glass casserole. Cook, covered, on HIGH 6 minutes. Stir in cheese and olives; cook, uncovered, on HIGH 1 minute. Serve over corn bread.*

Taco Franks

- 1 cup (4 oz.) shredded Cheddar cheese
- ½ cup crushed corn chips
- ½ cup finely chopped onion
- ¼ cup green chile salsa
- 6 Armour Star Dinner Franks, split lengthwise

Heat oven to 350°. Combine cheese, chips, onion and salsa. Stuff each frank with ¼ cup of mixture; place in 10 × 6-inch baking dish. Bake at 350°, 15 to 20 minutes.

6 servings

Chili Weather Peppers

- 4 green peppers
- ⅓ cup chopped onion
- ⅓ cup chopped celery
- 2 tablespoons butter or margarine
- 1 15½-oz. can Armour Star Chili with Beans
- 1 cup cooked rice
- ½ teaspoon salt
- ⅛ teaspoon garlic powder
- 2 slices (2 oz.) Swiss cheese, cut in strips

Heat oven to 375°. Remove tops and seeds from green peppers. Cook in boiling salted water 5 minutes; drain. Cook onion and celery in butter or margarine 10 minutes. Stir in chili, rice, salt and garlic powder; spoon mixture into peppers. Place stuffed peppers in 8-inch square baking dish. Bake at 375°, 25 minutes. Top with cheese strips; heat 5 minutes or until cheese melts.

4 servings

Fireside Chili Pot

  2 15½-oz. cans Armour Star Chili with Beans
  2 cups cooked rice
  ½ cup chopped onion
  ½ cup chopped green pepper
  ¼ cup sliced pitted ripe olives
  ½ cup (2 oz.) shredded Cheddar cheese

Combine chili, rice, onion and green pepper in large saucepan; heat over low heat, stirring occasionally, 20 minutes or until bubbly. Sprinkle with olives and cheese; continue heating until cheese melts, approximately 10 minutes.

6 servings

Microwave Instructions: *Combine chili, rice, onion and green pepper in 3-quart glass casserole. Cook, covered, on HIGH 12 minutes, stirring occasionally. Sprinkle with olives and cheese. Cook, covered, on HIGH 1 minute. Let stand, covered, 5 minutes before serving.*

Chili Plus

  1   15½-oz. can Armour Star Chili with Beans
  1½ cups cooked rice
  ¼   cup chopped onion
  ¼   cup chopped green pepper
  ½   cup (2 oz.) shredded process American cheese

Combine chili, rice, onion and green pepper in 2-quart saucepan; simmer, covered, 15 minutes. Sprinkle with cheese; cook on low heat until cheese melts.

4 servings

Bacon-Bean Bake

- 4 slices Armour Star Bacon
- ¼ cup chopped onion
- ¼ cup chopped green pepper
- 1 31-oz. can pork and beans in tomato sauce
- 2 tablespoons brown sugar, packed
- 2 tablespoons catsup
- 2 teaspoons Worcestershire sauce
- 1 teaspoon prepared mustard

In large fry pan, cook bacon 15 minutes. Remove from pan; chop. Cook onion and green pepper in bacon drippings 3 to 4 minutes. Add bacon and remaining ingredients. Heat, covered, on low heat 1 hour. Remove cover, stir; continue heating, uncovered, 30 minutes.

6 servings

Easy Barbecue Bean Bake

- 2 16-oz. cans baked beans
- 6 slices Armour Star Spiced Luncheon Meat
- ½ cup barbecue sauce

Heat oven to 350°. Place beans in 10x6-inch baking dish; place luncheon meat slices, slightly overlapping, down center. Spread with barbecue sauce. Bake at 350°, 20 to 25 minutes.

6 servings

Microwave Instructions: *Place beans in 10x6-inch glass baking dish; place luncheon meat slices, slightly overlapping, down center. Spread with barbecue sauce. Cover tightly with plastic wrap. Cook on HIGH 10 minutes, rotating dish halfway through cooking time. Let stand 5 minutes.*

Tangy Cream of Spinach Soup

  1   10-oz. package frozen chopped spinach, thawed
  2   tablespoons butter or margarine
2½   cups milk
  2   tablespoons flour
      Dash of thyme
      Dash of nutmeg
  1   cup diced Armour Star Salt Pork
¾   cup dairy sour cream

Combine spinach and butter or margarine in saucepan; cook, covered, 5 minutes. Pour into blender; add 1 cup milk. Blend until smooth. Add remaining milk, flour and seasonings; blend. Return mixture to saucepan; cook over medium heat, stirring occasionally until thickened, about 10 minutes. Fry salt pork until crisp and light brown; drain. Stir ¾ cup salt pork and ½ cup sour cream into soup; pour into bowls. Garnish with remaining salt pork and sour cream.

4 servings

Corn-Hash Muffins

  1   8½-oz. package corn muffin mix
  1   15-oz. can Armour Star Corned Beef Hash
½   cup finely chopped green onions and tops
½   cup grated Parmesan cheese
  1   egg
½   teaspoon salt
      Dash of pepper

Heat oven to 400°. Prepare corn muffin batter according to package directions; stir in remaining ingredients. Fill greased medium-size muffin pans, filling each cup ¾ full. Bake at 400°, 35 minutes or until golden brown.

12 muffins

Creamy Split Pea Soup

- 1 lb. dry split peas
- Water
- 1 1½- to 2-lb. Armour Star or 1877 Delite
- 1 cup chopped onion
- 2 tablespoons butter or margarine, melted
- 1 tablespoon flour
- 1 tablespoon salt
- ¼ teaspoon pepper
- ¼ cup milk

Soak peas in water overnight. Drain; rinse. Cover again with water; add Delite and onion. Simmer 1 hour and 45 minutes or until peas are tender. Remove Delite; cube. Drain peas, reserving liquid. Place peas and onion in blender; blend until smooth. Return to pan; combine with Delite cubes and 4 cups reserved liquid. Combine butter or margarine with flour, salt and pepper; add to pea mixture. Bring to a boil; reduce heat. Stir in milk; simmer 30 minutes.

8 servings

Vienna Sausage-Corn Chowder

- ¼ cup chopped onion
- ¼ cup butter or margarine
- ¼ cup flour
- 3 cups milk
- 2 5-oz. cans Armour Star Vienna Sausage in Beef Stock, drained, sliced
- 1 17-oz. can cream-style corn
- 1 tablespoon chopped parsley
- 1 tablespoon chopped pimiento
- 1 teaspoon salt
- ¼ teaspoon pepper

Cook onion in butter or margarine until tender; blend in flour. Add milk; cook, stirring constantly until thickened. Add remaining ingredients; heat.

5 cups

Potato-Dried Beef Chowder

1 cup finely chopped onion
¼ cup butter or margarine
¼ cup flour
4 cups milk
1 15-oz. can whole potatoes, drained, diced
1 5-oz. jar Armour Star Sliced Dried Beef, rinsed, chopped
1 tablespoon chopped parsley

In large saucepan, cook onion in butter or margarine until tender; stir in flour. Slowly add milk, stirring until thickened. Add potatoes and dried beef; heat, covered, on low heat 30 minutes. Top with parsley.

6 cups

Oriental Turkey Soup

1 10½-oz. can cut asparagus, drained, reserving liquid
2 14½-oz. cans chicken broth
1 2½-oz. jar sliced mushrooms, drained
½ cup coarsely chopped onion
2 tablespoons cornstarch
2 tablespoons cold water
2 cups chopped cooked Armour Golden Star Boneless Young Turkey
Dash of pepper
1½ cups shredded lettuce

In large saucepan, combine reserved asparagus liquid, broth, mushrooms and onion. Simmer, covered, 7 minutes. Combine cornstarch with water; stir into broth mixture. Simmer, stirring occasionally, until bubbly. Stir in turkey, asparagus and pepper; heat through. Place ¼ cup lettuce in each soup bowl; pour soup over lettuce.

6 servings

Turkey Quiche

- 1 cup chopped cooked Armour Golden Star Boneless Young Turkey
- 1 2½-oz. jar sliced mushrooms, drained
- 1 9-inch unbaked pastry shell
- 1½ cups (6 oz.) shredded Swiss cheese
- 2 tablespoons flour
- 4 eggs, slightly beaten
- 1½ cups milk
- ½ teaspoon salt
- ⅛ teaspoon ground red pepper

Heat oven to 350°. Place turkey and mushrooms in pastry shell. Toss cheese with flour; add to pastry shell. Combine eggs, milk and seasonings; pour into pastry shell. Bake at 350°, 40 to 45 minutes.

6 servings

Hot Crunchy Turkey Cups

- 2 cups chopped cooked Armour Golden Star Boneless Young Turkey
- 2 cups chopped celery
- 1 cup mayonnaise
- ½ cup chopped almonds, toasted
- 2 tablespoons lemon juice
- 2 teaspoons grated onion
- ½ teaspoon salt
- ½ cup (2 oz.) shredded Cheddar cheese
- 1 cup crushed potato chips

Heat oven to 450°. Combine all ingredients except cheese and potato chips; mix lightly. Spoon into six 6-ounce custard cups. Sprinkle with cheese and potato chips. Bake at 450°, 10 minutes.

6 servings

Vienna Biscuit Ring

- 1 can refrigerated buttermilk biscuits (10 biscuits)
- 2 5-oz. cans Armour Star Vienna Sausage in Beef Stock, drained
- 2 tablespoons butter or margarine
- 2 tablespoons flour
- ½ teaspoon salt
- 1 cup milk
- 1 10-oz. package frozen mixed vegetables, cooked according to package directions
- ¼ cup dairy sour cream
- ½ teaspoon Worcestershire sauce

Heat oven to 400°. Flatten biscuits; place in a ring, slightly overlapping, on greased cookie sheet. Put 1 sausage in center of each biscuit. Bake at 400°, 15 minutes. Thinly slice remaining sausages. Melt butter or margarine; stir in flour and salt. Slowly add milk, stirring until thickened. Combine sauce, vegetables, sour cream, Worcestershire sauce and remaining sausages; heat. Remove biscuit ring to platter; fill center with vegetable mixture.

5 servings

Viennese Rarebit

- 1 8-oz. jar process cheese spread
- ¼ cup milk
- 1 5-oz. can Armour Star Vienna Sausage in Beef Stock, drained, thinly sliced
- 2 tablespoons grated onion
- 2 cups hot cooked rice

Heat cheese and milk over medium-low heat; stir until smooth. Add sausages and onion. Serve over rice.

4 servings

Florentine Chopped Ham

¼ cup butter or margarine
¼ cup flour
½ teaspoon salt
Dash of pepper
2 cups milk
1 tablespoon prepared mustard
1 12-oz. can Armour Star Chopped Ham, cubed
1 10-oz. package frozen chopped spinach, cooked according to package directions
1 2½-oz. jar sliced mushrooms, drained
6 frozen patty shells, baked according to package directions

Melt butter or margarine; stir in flour, salt and pepper. Slowly add milk, stirring until thickened. Stir in mustard, chopped ham, spinach and mushrooms; heat thoroughly. Serve in patty shells.

6 servings

Microwave Instructions: Melt butter or margarine in 2-quart glass casserole. Stir in flour, salt, pepper and milk. Cook, covered, on HIGH 6 minutes, stirring occasionally. Stir in mustard, chopped ham, spinach and mushrooms; cook, covered, on HIGH 2 minutes. Serve in patty shells.

Scalloped Delite

1 5½-oz. package scalloped potatoes
1 1-lb. Armour Star or 1877 Delite, sliced in ¼-inch slices

Heat oven to 400°. In 2-quart casserole, prepare potatoes according to package directions; stir in Delite. Bake, uncovered, at 400°, 30 to 35 minutes.

4 servings

Saucy Fiesta

- 2 cups cubed Armour Star Spiced Luncheon Meat
- ½ cup chopped green pepper
- ½ cup chopped onion
- 2 tablespoons butter or margarine
- 1 11-oz. can Cheddar cheese soup
- ⅓ cup milk
- 4 white bread slices, toasted, cut in quarters

Cook spiced luncheon meat, green pepper and onion in butter or margarine until meat is brown. Add soup and milk; stir. Heat to bubbling. Serve on toast points.

4 servings

Hawaiian Beef Kabobs

- 1 1½-lb. Naturally Tender Beef Top Round Steak, cut in ¼ × 4- inch strips
- ⅔ cup soy sauce
- ⅓ cup lemon juice
- ⅓ cup vegetable oil
- 1 tablespoon dry mustard
- 1 teaspoon ginger
- ¼ teaspoon garlic powder
- ¼ teaspoon pepper
- 12 cherry tomatoes
- 12 green pepper chunks
- 12 mushrooms

Place beef in shallow dish. Combine soy sauce, lemon juice, oil, dry mustard, ginger, garlic powder and pepper; pour over beef. Cover; marinate in refrigerator 6 hours, turning occasionally. Drain beef, reserving marinade. On 6 metal skewers, thread beef accordian style, alternating with tomatoes, green pepper and mushrooms. Brush with marinade. Grill over hot coals or broil, 5 to 7 minutes on each side, brushing occasionally with marinade.

6 servings

Crunchy Garden-Ham Bake

- 3 cups cubed Armour Star Chopped Ham
- 3 cups shredded cabbage
- 1 cup sliced celery
- ¼ cup chopped green onions
- 1 10¾-oz. can cream of mushroom soup

Heat oven to 350°. Combine all ingredients; place in 2-quart casserole. Bake, covered, at 350°, 50 minutes.

6 servings

Microwave Instructions: *Combine all ingredients in 2-quart glass casserole. Cook, covered, on HIGH 15 minutes, stirring occasionally. Let stand 5 minutes.*

Zucchini-Beef Bake

- 4 zucchini, cut in ¼-inch slices
- 1 cup chopped onion
- ½ cup chopped celery
- 2 tablespoons vegetable oil
- 1 lb. Naturally Tender Ground Beef
- 1 cup sliced mushrooms
- 1 6-oz. can tomato paste
- ¼ cup red wine
- 1 teaspoon salt
- ½ teaspoon oregano
- ¼ teaspoon pepper
- 2 cups (8 oz.) shredded Mozzarella cheese

Heat oven to 350°. Arrange zucchini in 13 × 9-inch baking dish. In fry pan, cook onion and celery in oil 5 minutes. Add ground beef; cook until beef loses pink color. Stir in mushrooms, tomato paste, wine and seasonings; simmer 5 minutes. Spoon cooked mixture over zucchini; sprinkle with cheese. Bake at 350°, 25 minutes or until cheese is light brown.

6 servings

Beef and Tangy 'Taters

- 1 5-oz. jar Armour Star Sliced Dried Beef, chopped
- ¾ cup chopped onion
- ¼ cup butter or margarine
- 3 tablespoons flour
- 2 tablespoons sugar
- ⅓ cup vinegar
- ⅓ cup water
- ½ cup mayonnaise
- 1 tablespoon chopped parsley
- 1 teaspoon celery salt
- 4 cups chopped cooked potatoes

Heat oven to 375°. In fry pan, cook dried beef and onion in butter or margarine on medium heat 10 minutes. Stir in flour and sugar. Gradually add vinegar and water; cook, stirring constantly until thickened. Remove from heat; stir in mayonnaise, parsley and celery salt. Gently fold in potatoes. Place in 2-quart casserole. Bake, covered, at 375°, 30 to 35 minutes.

4 servings

Beef Romanoff

- 6 tablespoons butter or margarine
- 6 tablespoons flour
- 1½ cups milk
- ½ cup dry white wine
- 1 14-oz. can artichoke hearts, drained, cut in half
- 1 2½-oz. jar Armour Star Sliced Dried Beef, cut in strips
- 1 cup dairy sour cream
- Hot cooked noodles

In fry pan, melt butter or margarine on medium-low heat; blend in flour. Gradually add milk; cook, stirring until thickened. Stir in wine, artichokes and dried beef. Cook 10 minutes. Gently fold in sour cream. Serve over noodles.

5 to 6 servings

Saucy Broccoli Crêpes

- ⅔ cup finely chopped Armour Star Salt Pork
- ½ cup finely chopped onion
- 2 tablespoons flour
- ½ cup milk
- 1 teaspoon Armour Star Chicken Flavor Instant Bouillon or 1 Armour Star Chicken Flavor Bouillon cube dissolved in ½ cup boiling water
- 1 10-oz. package frozen chopped broccoli, cooked according to package directions, drained
- 6 Crêpes (page 143), heated

Fry salt pork until crisp and light brown; remove from pan, reserving 2 tablespoons drippings. Cook onion 5 minutes or until tender; blend in flour. Gradually add milk and bouillon; cook, stirring constantly until thickened. Add broccoli and salt pork. Fill crêpes; roll.

6 crêpes

Beef à la Reine

- 1 2½-oz. jar Armour Star Sliced Dried Beef, cut in strips
- 2 cups sliced mushrooms
- 2 tablespoons finely chopped onion
- ¼ cup butter or margarine
- ¼ cup flour
- 1¼ cups milk
- 1 cup dairy sour cream
- 1 cup (4 oz.) shredded Cheddar cheese
- Hot cooked asparagus spears

In fry pan, cook dried beef, mushrooms and onion in butter or margarine on medium heat 5 minutes; blend in flour. Gradually add milk; cook, stirring until thickened. Stir in sour cream; sprinkle with cheese. Cover pan; allow to cook over low heat 5 minutes or until cheese melts. Stir lightly. Serve over asparagus.

5 to 6 servings

Main Dishes

What's the secret of a memorable meal? A special main dish, with Armour magic. Best of all, it's easy to conjure up! Fragrant stews with a luscious slow-simmered flavor make an appearance in minutes. Whole-meal casseroles are ready in about as much time as it takes to set the table. And part of that just-the-right-size little ham returns for a curtain call the next day in another interesting dish. So easy, it seems like sorcery . . . so convenient, it must be Armour.

New England Sausage Dinner

- 1 lb. Armour Star Polish Sausage
- 4 medium potatoes, peeled, quartered
- 4 large carrots, cut in 1-inch pieces
- 1 small head cabbage, quartered
- 2 cups water
- 2 tablespoons flour
- 2 tablespoons brown sugar, packed
- 2 tablespoons vinegar
- 1 teaspoon dry mustard
- ½ teaspoon salt
- ½ teaspoon pepper
- Chopped parsley

Place sausage in large saucepan; add potatoes, carrots, cabbage and water. Cook, covered, 30 minutes or until vegetables are tender. Place sausage and vegetables on platter; keep warm. Reserve broth. Combine ¾ cup reserved broth with flour, brown sugar, vinegar, dry mustard, salt and pepper. Cook until thickened, stirring constantly. Serve over sausage and vegetables. Garnish with parsley.

4 servings

Apple 'n Sauerkraut Sausage

 1 lb. Armour Star Kulbassy, cut in 1-inch pieces
 1 27-oz. can sauerkraut, drained
 1 cup chopped apple
 ¼ cup brown sugar, packed
 ¼ cup water
 ½ teaspoon caraway seed

Combine all ingredients in fry pan; cover. Simmer 30 minutes or until heated through.

6 servings

Microwave Instructions: *Combine all ingredients in 2-quart glass casserole. Cook, covered, on HIGH 8 to 10 minutes, stirring occasionally. Let stand, covered, 2 minutes.*

Kulbassy-Potato Combo

 6 cups chopped cooked potatoes
 2 hard-cooked eggs, sliced
 2 tablespoons sliced green onions
 1 lb. Armour Star Kulbassy, thinly sliced
 6 slices Armour Star Bacon, chopped
 3 tablespoons sugar
 1 tablespoon cornstarch
 1 tablespoon salt
 ¾ cup water
 ⅓ cup vinegar

Combine potatoes, eggs and green onions; set aside. Brown sausage; add to potato mixture. Cook bacon until crisp. Combine sugar, cornstarch, salt, water and vinegar; slowly add to bacon, stirring constantly until thickened. Pour over potato mixture; toss lightly.

6 servings

Paul Bunyan Sausage Supper

- 1 lb. Armour Star Smoked Sausage
- 1 16-oz. can sauerkraut
- 1 15-oz. can potatoes
- 1 cup onion chunks
- 1 teaspoon salt
- Paprika
- Chopped parsley

Combine sausage, sauerkraut, potatoes, onion and salt in large saucepan. Cook, covered, over medium heat 30 minutes. Serve on platter; garnish with paprika and parsley.

4 servings

Microwave Instructions: Combine sauerkraut, potatoes and onion in 3-quart glass casserole. Cook, covered, on HIGH 5 minutes. Add sausage; cook, covered, on HIGH 10 minutes. Stir in salt; garnish with paprika and parsley.

Spaghetti-Sausage Supper

- 2 28-oz. cans whole peeled tomatoes
- 1 1½-oz. envelope spaghetti sauce mix
- 1 lb. Armour Star Kulbassy, cut in ½-inch pieces
- ½ lb. spaghetti, broken in half
- 1 cup sliced celery
- ½ cup chopped onion
- Grated Parmesan cheese

In large fry pan, pour in tomatoes and juice; cut tomatoes in large pieces. Stir in sauce mix. Add sausage, spaghetti, celery and onion; bring to a boil. Reduce heat to low. Cook, covered, 25 to 30 minutes, stirring occasionally, until spaghetti is tender. Serve with cheese.

6 to 8 servings

Skillet Sausage Sweets

- ¼ cup finely chopped onion
- ¼ cup butter or margarine
- 2 tablespoons flour
- 1 15¼-oz. can pineapple chunks, drained, reserving syrup
- ⅓ cup water
- ⅓ cup brown sugar, packed
- 1 lb. Armour Star Polish Sausage, cut in 1-inch pieces
- 3 cups sliced cooked sweet potato

Cook onion in butter or margarine 2 to 3 minutes; stir in flour. Add reserved syrup and water; cook, stirring constantly until thickened. Stir in pineapple, brown sugar and sausage. Top with sweet potatoes. Cook, covered, 15 to 20 minutes or until heated.

4 servings

Microwave Instructions: *Melt butter or margarine in 3-quart glass casserole; stir in onion and flour. Add reserved syrup and water. Cook, covered, on HIGH 3 minutes. Stir in pineapple, brown sugar, sausage and sweet potatoes. Cook, covered, on HIGH 8 to 9 minutes. Let stand, covered, 2 minutes.*

Hot Dog Crescents

- 1 8-oz. package refrigerated crescent dinner rolls
  Prepared mustard
- 8 Armour Star Hot Dogs

Heat oven to 375°. Separate dough into 8 triangles; spread with mustard. Place each hot dog on dough triangle; roll as for crescent rolls. Place on ungreased cookie sheet. Bake at 375°, 18 to 20 minutes.

4 servings

Hot Dog Splits

    1 cup hot cooked mashed potatoes
    1 cup (4 oz.) shredded Cheddar cheese
    ¼ cup chopped onion
    ½ teaspoon salt
    8 Armour Star Hot Dogs, split lengthwise

Heat oven to 400°. Combine potatoes, cheese, onion and salt. Stuff each hot dog with 2 tablespoons of mixture; place in 13 × 9-inch baking dish. Bake at 400°, 15 to 20 minutes.

4 servings

Family Hot Dog Supper

    1 lb. Armour Star Hot Dogs, sliced in ½-inch pieces
    1 14-oz. package macaroni and cheese deluxe dinner, prepared according to package directions
    ¼ cup finely chopped onion
    ¼ cup finely chopped green pepper
      Dash of pepper
      Sweet red pepper rings

Heat oven to 350°. Combine all ingredients except red pepper; mix well. Pour into 2-quart casserole. Bake, uncovered, at 350°, 25 to 30 minutes. Garnish with red pepper.

6 to 8 servings

Microwave Instructions: *Combine all ingredients except red pepper; mix well. Pour into 2-quart glass casserole. Cook, covered, on HIGH 6½ to 7 minutes, stirring halfway through cooking time. Let stand, covered, 2 minutes. Garnish with red pepper.*

Franks 'n Hot Potato Salad

2 15½-oz. cans German potato salad
4 Armour Star Dinner Franks

Spoon potato salad into fry pan; top with franks. Cook, covered, on medium heat 20 minutes.

4 servings

Microwave Instructions: *Spoon potato salad into 10 × 6-inch glass baking dish; top with franks. Cook, covered, on HIGH 7 to 7½ minutes, rotating dish halfway through cooking time. Let stand, covered, 2 minutes.*

Franks 'n Kraut Goulash

½ cup chopped onion
3 tablespoons butter or margarine
6 Armour Star Dinner Franks, cut in half lengthwise
1 27-oz. can sauerkraut, drained
1 cup dairy sour cream
1 teaspoon sugar
½ teaspoon caraway seed
½ teaspoon paprika
¼ teaspoon salt

Cook onion in butter or margarine 5 minutes. Add franks and sauerkraut; heat, covered, 15 minutes. Stir in remaining ingredients; continue heating, uncovered, 5 minutes.

6 servings

Franks 'n Hot Potato Salad

Tangy Kabobs

1 12-oz. can Armour Star Treet luncheon meat, cut in 1-inch cubes
2 green peppers, cut in chunks
1 16-oz. can small whole onions
12 cherry tomatoes
12 fresh mushrooms
1 cup sweet and sour sauce

Arrange Treet, green peppers, onions, cherry tomatoes and mushrooms on skewers. Place skewers on grill; brush with sauce. Heat 10 minutes, turning and brushing occasionally with sauce.

4 servings

Pantry-Shelf Casserole

1 12-oz. can Armour Star Treet luncheon meat, cut into ½-inch cubes
¼ cup butter or margarine
¼ cup flour
½ teaspoon salt
1 14½-oz. can stewed tomatoes
1 16-oz. can green lima beans, drained
½ cup (2 oz.) shredded Cheddar cheese

Heat oven to 325°. Brown Treet in butter or margarine; blend in flour and salt. Add tomatoes; cook, stirring constantly, until thickened. Add beans; mix well. Pour into 10 × 6-inch baking dish; sprinkle with cheese. Bake at 325°, 20 minutes.

4 servings

Bacon-Macaroni Casserole

- 1 cup dairy sour cream
- ½ cup grated Parmesan cheese
- ½ teaspoon salt
- ¼ teaspoon paprika
- 2 cups cooked elbow macaroni
- 1 lb. Armour Star Bacon, crisply cooked, quartered
- 2 cups soft bread crumbs
- ¼ cup butter or margarine, melted

Combine sour cream, cheese, salt and paprika in saucepan; stir in hot macaroni. Heat, covered, over low heat 5 minutes or until heated through. Stir in bacon. Pour mixture into 10 × 6-inch baking dish. Combine bread crumbs and butter or margarine; sprinkle over top. Broil 3 to 5 minutes or until crumbs are brown.

6 servings

Easy Skillet Scallop

- 1 cup cubed Armour Star Salt Pork
- Cornmeal
- 3 cups sliced potatoes
- 3 cups sliced onions
- 2 tablespoons flour
- ¼ teaspoon pepper
- 1 13-oz. can evaporated milk

Coat salt pork with cornmeal; brown lightly in fry pan. Remove salt pork from pan. Layer ½ potatoes, salt pork, onions, remaining potatoes, flour, pepper and milk. Cook, covered, over low heat, 1 hour or until potatoes are tender.

4 servings

Stuffed Pork Chops

- 4 Veribest Pork Loin Rib Chops, cut 1½-inches thick
- 1 cup finely chopped apple
- 1 cup soft bread crumbs
- ½ cup chicken broth
- ¼ cup chopped onion
- ¼ cup raisins
- 2 tablespoons chopped parsley
- ½ teaspoon salt

Heat oven to 350°. Make pocket in each chop by cutting between rib bones. Combine remaining ingredients; mix well. Stuff each chop with ½ cup stuffing mixture. Place in 12 × 8-inch baking dish. Bake at 350°, 1 hour and 15 minutes, turning once during baking.

4 servings

Savory Stuffed Potatoes

- 4 large baking potatoes
- ½ cup dairy sour cream
- 1 teaspoon salt
-   Dash of pepper
- 8 slices Armour Star Bacon, cut in 1-inch pieces
- ½ cup chopped onion
- ¼ cup chopped green pepper
- 1 cup (4 oz.) shredded Cheddar cheese

Heat oven to 400°. Scrub potatoes; prick with fork. Bake at 400°, 1 hour. Remove potatoes from oven. Cut a slice from top of each potato; scoop out potato into bowl. Add sour cream, salt and pepper; mash until fluffy. Cook bacon until almost crisp; add onion and green pepper. Cook 5 minutes; drain. Stir bacon, onion, green pepper and cheese into potato mixture. Pile mixture lightly into potato shells. Bake at 400°, 10 minutes.

4 servings

Sausage Fried Rice

- 2 5-oz. cans Armour Star Vienna Sausage in Beef Stock, sliced diagonally in thirds
- 1 2½-oz. jar sliced mushrooms, drained
- ½ cup sliced green onions and tops
- ¼ cup vegetable oil
- 3 cups cooked rice
- 2 tablespoons soy sauce
- ½ teaspoon salt
- 2 eggs, beaten

In a wok or large fry pan, cook sausages, mushrooms and green onions in oil over medium heat 5 minutes; stir in rice, soy sauce and salt. Heat, stirring occasionally, 8 to 10 minutes. Reduce heat; stir in eggs. Cook, stirring constantly until eggs are cooked. Serve immediately.

6 servings

New Orleans Jambalaya

- ¼ cup chopped onion
- 2 tablespoons butter or margarine
- 1 cup cubed Armour's Pork Shoulder Picnic
- 1 cup cooked shrimp
- 1½ cups cooked rice
- 1 cup hot water
- 3 tablespoons tomato paste
- 2 tablespoons chopped parsley
- 1½ teaspoons flour
- ¼ teaspoon garlic powder
- Pitted ripe olives

Cook onion in butter or margarine 5 minutes. Stir in remaining ingredients. Cook over low heat 10 minutes or until thoroughly heated. Garnish with olives.

4 servings

Spaghetti alla Carbonara

- 8 slices Armour Star Bacon, diced
- 4 cloves garlic, crushed
- ¼ cup dry white wine
- 3 eggs, beaten
- ¾ cup grated Parmesan cheese
- 2 tablespoons chopped parsley
- ¼ teaspoon pepper
- 5 quarts water
- 1 tablespoon salt
- 1 lb. spaghetti

In a large fry pan, cook bacon until crisp. Add garlic; cook 1 to 2 minutes. Add wine to fry pan, stirring until wine boils away; remove from heat. In a large serving bowl, combine eggs, cheese, parsley and pepper. In a large pan, bring water and salt to a boil; add spaghetti. Cook until tender; drain well. Add hot spaghetti to large serving bowl containing egg mixture. Toss rapidly until spaghetti is well coated; pour in hot bacon mixture. Toss again; serve immediately.

4 servings

Delite à l'Orange

- 2 cups water
- 1 cup rice
- ¼ cup frozen orange juice concentrate
- 2 tablespoons raisins
- 2 tablespoons slivered almonds
- ½ teaspoon salt
- Dash of pepper
- 1 1- to 1½-lb. Armour Star or 1877 Delite

Heat oven to 325°. Combine all ingredients except Delite in 3-quart casserole. Place Delite on top. Bake, covered, at 325°, 1 hour and 15 minutes to 1 hour and 30 minutes, stirring rice halfway through cooking time.

4 to 6 servings

Apricot Pork Roast

- 1 3- to 4-lb. Veribest Pork Loin Roast
- ½ cup apricot nectar
- ¼ cup brown sugar, packed
- 1 16-oz. can apricot halves, drained, reserving syrup
- 2 teaspoons vinegar

Heat oven to 325°. Roast pork at 325°, 2 hours and 30 minutes or until meat thermometer registers 170°. Combine apricot nectar, brown sugar, apricot syrup and vinegar. Brush pork with glaze during last 30 minutes of roasting time. Arrange apricots around roast on serving platter.

6 to 8 servings

Roast Leg-O-Pork with Potato Medley

- 1 4- to 5-lb. Veribest Boneless Leg-O-Pork (Fresh Ham)
- 2 large yams, cut in ½-inch slices
- 3 large potatoes, peeled, quartered
- 3 cups water
- ⅓ cup cornstarch
- 1 cup cold water
- Salt
- Pepper

Heat oven to 325°. Roast pork at 325°, 3 hours or until meat thermometer registers 170°. Cook yams and potatoes in boiling salted water for 8 minutes; drain. Peel yams. Arrange yams and potatoes around pork during last 30 to 40 minutes. For gravy, pour off all but ½ cup drippings. Add 3 cups water. Moisten cornstarch with 1 cup cold water. Add to drippings; cook, stirring constantly until thickened. Season with salt and pepper.

6 to 8 servings

Mincemeat-Glazed Ham

- 1 5-lb. Golden Star Ham by Armour
- 1 cup mincemeat
- 1 cup apple cider
- 2 teaspoons grated lemon rind
- 1 tablespoon cornstarch
  Lemons
  Mint sprigs

Heat ham according to label instructions. Combine mincemeat, ¾ cup apple cider and lemon rind. Moisten cornstarch with ¼ cup apple cider; add to mincemeat mixture. Cook, stirring constantly, until thickened. Spoon mincemeat glaze over ham during last 30 minutes of heating time. Cut thin slice from end of each lemon. Starting at cut end, cut a thin spiral peel in a continuous motion. Curl peel to resemble a rose; secure with wooden pick. Place heated ham on platter. Garnish with lemon-peel roses and mint.

Plum Nuts Ham

- 1 1½-lb. Armour Star Ham
- ½ cup plum jelly
- 2 teaspoons chopped pecans
- 2 teaspoons grated orange rind

Heat ham according to label instructions. Combine remaining ingredients; spread over ham during last 20 minutes of heating.

Ham Fritters

　1　egg, beaten
　½　cup milk
　¼　cup finely chopped onion
　1　teaspoon Worcestershire sauce
　　　Dash of Tabasco sauce
　2　cups buttermilk baking mix
1½　cups diced Golden Star Ham by Armour
　　　Vegetable oil, heated
　　　Tart jelly

Combine egg, milk, onion, Worcestershire sauce and Tabasco sauce; add baking mix. Stir in ham. Drop by tablespoons into deep hot oil, 365°, 5 to 7 minutes or until golden brown. Drain on absorbent paper. Serve with jelly.

4 servings

Magic Cherry Ham

1　1½-lb. Golden Star Ham by Armour
¼　cup cherry preserves

Heat oven to 325°. Bake ham according to label instructions. After first 30 minutes, spoon preserves over ham; continue baking 30 minutes.

6 servings

Microwave Instructions: Remove "zip-top" lid from plastic ham container. Cover with wax paper. Cook on HIGH 12 minutes, rotating container twice during cooking time. Spoon preserves over ham. Cook, uncovered, on HIGH 3 minutes. Let stand 5 minutes.

Orange Blossom Ham

- 1 5- to 8-lb. Armour Star Boneless Ham
- ½ cup brown sugar, packed
- 1 tablespoon cornstarch
- ¼ teaspoon ground cloves
-    Dash of ginger
- ½ cup orange juice

Heat ham according to label instructions. Combine brown sugar, cornstarch, cloves and ginger; add orange juice. Heat, stirring constantly, until thickened. Spoon glaze over ham during last 30 minutes of heating.

Peach-Glazed Ham Loaf

- 3 cups ground Armour Star Boneless Ham
- ½ cup dry bread crumbs
- 2 eggs, slightly beaten
- 5 tablespoons lemon juice
- ¼ cup finely chopped green pepper
- 2 tablespoons brown sugar, packed
- 2 tablespoons finely chopped onion
- 1 tablespoon prepared mustard
- ¼ cup peach preserves

Heat oven to 350°. In large bowl, combine all ingredients except preserves and 3 tablespoons lemon juice. In shallow baking pan, shape mixture into loaf; bake at 350°, 30 minutes. In small bowl, combine preserves and remaining lemon juice. Remove loaf from oven; spoon glaze over loaf. Bake 15 minutes longer. Let stand 15 minutes before slicing.

6 servings

Stew 'n Corn Bread Casserole

- 1 cup green pepper, cut in ½-inch chunks
- 2 tablespoons butter or margarine
- 1 24-oz. can Armour Star Beef Stew
- 1 15-oz. can kidney beans, drained
- 1 8¼-oz. can tomatoes, chopped, drained
- 2 tablespoons chili powder
- 1 15-oz. package corn bread mix, mixed according to package directions

Heat oven to 425°. Cook green pepper in butter or margarine 5 minutes; drain. Combine green pepper, stew, kidney beans, tomatoes and chili powder; pour into lightly greased 13 × 9-inch baking dish. Spread corn bread mix on top. Bake at 425°, 20 minutes.

6 to 8 servings

Far East Beef Stew

- 1 24-oz. can Armour Star Beef Stew
- 1 8½-oz. can water chestnuts, drained, sliced
- ½ cup green onions and tops, cut in 1-inch pieces
- ¼ cup soy sauce
- ⅛ teaspoon ground ginger
- Hot cooked rice
- Chow mein noodles

In fry pan, combine stew, water chestnuts, green onions, soy sauce and ginger; simmer 10 minutes. Serve over rice. Garnish with noodles.

4 servings

Beef Stew with Parsley Dumplings

- 2 24-oz. cans Armour Star Beef Stew
- 2 cups buttermilk baking mix
- 2 tablespoons chopped parsley
- ⅔ cup milk

Heat oven to 425°. Place stew in 3-quart casserole. Bake, covered, at 425°, 10 minutes. Combine baking mix, parsley and milk. Drop by spoonfuls on top of stew. Continue baking, covered, 20 to 25 minutes.

6 servings

Microwave Instructions: *Place stew in 3-quart glass casserole. Cook, covered, on HIGH 10 minutes, stirring occasionally. Combine baking mix, parsley and milk. Drop by spoonfuls on top of stew. Cook, covered, on HIGH 6 to 8 minutes or until dumplings are no longer doughy underneath.*

Chili Strata

- 1 egg, slightly beaten
- ¾ cup water
- 1 12-oz. package corn chips
- 2 15½-oz. cans Armour Star Chili with Beans
- 1 19-oz. can enchilada sauce
- ¾ cup chopped green pepper
- ⅓ cup chopped onion
- 2 cups (8 oz.) shredded Cheddar cheese
- 4 cups chopped lettuce
- 2 cups chopped tomatoes

Heat oven to 350°. Mix egg and water. Crush 4 cups corn chips to make 2 cups crushed chips. Add egg mixture to crushed chips; spread in lightly greased 13 × 9-inch baking dish. Combine chili, 1 cup enchilada sauce, green pepper and onion; spread over corn chips in casserole. Bake at 350°, 35 minutes. Top with cheese and remaining whole corn chips; bake 5 minutes. Top with lettuce and tomatoes. Serve with sauce.

6 to 8 servings

Chuck Wagon Steak

- 1   1½- to 2-lb. Naturally Tender Beef Blade Steak, cut ¾ to 1 inch thick
- 1   cup chopped onion
- 1   cup catsup
- ⅓   cup vinegar
- 2   tablespoons brown sugar, packed
- 2   teaspoons salt
- 1   teaspoon garlic salt
- 1   bay leaf
- ⅛   teaspoon hot pepper sauce

Place steak in shallow dish. Combine remaining ingredients in saucepan; simmer 10 minutes. Cool sauce; pour over steak, coating all sides. Cover; marinate in refrigerator 8 hours, turning occasionally. Remove steak, reserving marinade. Broil steak, 4 inches from heat, 15 minutes on each side, brushing occasionally with marinade.

4 servings

Beef 'n Cheese Strata

- ½   cup finely chopped onion
- ½   cup finely chopped celery
- 2   tablespoons butter or margarine
- 12 white bread slices, crusts trimmed
- 1   12-oz. can Armour Star Chopped Beef, sliced into 12 slices
- 1   cup (4 oz.) shredded Cheddar cheese
- 3   eggs, beaten
- 1½ cups milk
- 1   teaspoon salt
    Dash of pepper

Heat oven to 350°. Cook onion and celery in butter or margarine 5 minutes. In a greased 12 × 8-inch baking dish, layer bread, chopped beef slices, onion and celery mixture and cheese; repeat. Mix together eggs, milk and seasonings; pour over casserole. Bake at 350°, 40 minutes. Let stand 5 minutes.

6 servings

Sloppy Joes Potatoes

- 4 large baking potatoes
- 1 15½-oz. can Armour Star Sloppy Joes, heated
- 1 cup (4 oz.) shredded Cheddar cheese

Heat oven to 400°. Scrub potatoes; prick with fork. Bake at 400°, 1 hour. Remove potatoes from oven. Cut crisscross gash in potato tops; squeeze gently until potato pops up through opening. Pour ⅓ cup sloppy Joes on each potato; top each with ¼ cup cheese. Return to oven; bake until cheese melts.

4 servings

Beef 'n Mac Casserole

- 1 5-oz. jar Armour Star Sliced Dried Beef, chopped in 1-inch pieces
- ½ cup sliced green onions
- ⅓ cup chopped celery
- 5 tablespoons butter or margarine, melted
- 2 cups cooked elbow macaroni
- 2 10¾-oz. cans cream of mushroom soup
- 2 cups milk
- ½ cup chopped green pepper
- 1 tablespoon Worcestershire sauce
- Dash of pepper
- 1 cup soft bread crumbs

Heat oven to 350°. In fry pan, cook dried beef, green onions and celery in 3 tablespoons butter or margarine on medium heat 5 minutes. Remove from heat; combine with macaroni, soup, milk, green pepper, Worcestershire sauce and pepper. Pour mixture into greased 13 × 9-inch baking dish. Bake at 350°, 55 minutes. Toss bread crumbs with remaining butter or margarine; sprinkle on top of casserole. Continue baking 5 minutes.

8 servings

Chili-Stuffed Zucchini

- 6 zucchini, cut in half lengthwise
- ⅓ cup chopped onion
- 1 tablespoon butter or margarine
- 1 15-oz. can Armour Star Chili—No Beans
- 1 cup cooked rice
- ¼ cup sliced pitted ripe olives
- ¼ cup grated Parmesan cheese
- ½ teaspoon salt
- ⅛ teaspoon garlic powder
- 2 slices (2 oz.) Mozzarella cheese, cut in strips

Heat oven to 375°. Scoop out seeds and pulp from squash. Cook onion in butter or margarine 10 minutes. Stir in chili, rice, olives, Parmesan cheese, salt and garlic powder. Spoon chili mixture into squash; arrange in 13 × 9-inch baking dish. Bake at 375°, 40 minutes. Top with cheese strips; heat 5 minutes or until cheese melts.

6 servings

Corned Beef and Cabbage

- 1 3- to 5-lb. Armour Star Corned Beef, Brisket or Round
- 1 bunch parsley, bound together
- 3 onions, cut in chunks
- 2 carrots, quartered
- 1 bay leaf
- ½ teaspoon pepper
- 2 heads cabbage, cut in wedges

Place corned beef in pan; cover with water. Add parsley, onions, carrots, bay leaf and pepper. Bring to a boil; reduce heat. Simmer, covered, 2 to 3 hours or until fork-tender. Remove meat; remove and discard parsley and bay leaf. Add cabbage; simmer 15 minutes or until cabbage is tender. Serve on platter with corned beef.

8 servings

Cheesy Corned Beef-Cabbage Casserole

- 14 cups cabbage, cut in 1-inch pieces
- 1 12-oz. can Armour Star Corned Beef, chopped
- 1 11-oz. can Cheddar cheese soup
- 1 5.33-oz. can evaporated milk
- 3 tablespoons grated onion
- 1 tablespoon prepared mustard
- ½ teaspoon salt
- 4 bread slices, cut into cubes
- 2 tablespoons butter or margarine, melted
- 4 slices process American cheese

Heat oven to 350°. In covered saucepan, cook cabbage in small amount of boiling water 5 to 8 minutes or until tender; drain well. In greased 3-quart casserole, arrange alternate layers of cabbage and corned beef. Combine soup, milk, onion, mustard and salt; pour over corned beef and cabbage. Toss bread cubes in butter or margarine; arrange around edge of casserole. Bake at 350°, 35 minutes or until bubbly. Arrange cheese over center of casserole; bake 5 minutes or until cheese melts.

6 to 8 servings

Mexican Stack-Ups

- 12 corn tortillas
  Vegetable oil, heated
- 1 8-oz. package cream cheese, softened
- 1 4-oz. can chopped green chiles, drained
- 2 15½-oz. cans Armour Star Chili with Beans
- 1 cup chopped lettuce
- 1 cup chopped tomato
- ½ cup (2 oz.) shredded Cheddar cheese

Heat oven to 350°. Fry tortillas in oil until crisp; drain. Combine cream cheese and green chiles. Spread each tortilla with cheese mixture; top with chili. Stack tortillas into 4 stacks; place on 15½x10½-inch jelly roll pan. Bake at 350°, 20 minutes. Top with lettuce, tomato and Cheddar cheese.

4 servings

Hash Pie

- 2 15-oz. cans Armour Star Corned Beef Hash
- ½ cup soft bread crumbs
- 2 eggs, slightly beaten
- 1 10-oz. package frozen mixed vegetables, cooked according to package directions
- 1 10¾-oz. can cream of celery soup

Heat oven to 375°. Combine hash, bread crumbs and eggs; mix until well blended. Place in 9-inch pie plate. Bake at 375°, 30 minutes or until set. Combine vegetables and soup; heat. To serve, cut pie into wedges; top with vegetable sauce.

6 servings

Hash 'n Squash

- 2 acorn squash
- Salt
- Pepper
- 2 15-oz. cans Armour Star Corned Beef Hash
- ½ cup (2 oz.) shredded Cheddar cheese
- 4 green pepper strips

Heat oven to 350°. Rinse squash. Cut in half; remove seeds. Place cut side down in shallow baking dish. Bake at 350°, 30 minutes. Turn squash cut side up; season with salt and pepper. Spoon hash into squash halves; heat 20 minutes. Sprinkle with cheese; continue heating until cheese melts, about 5 minutes. Garnish with green pepper strips.

4 servings

Microwave Instructions: *Rinse squash; leave whole. Cook on HIGH 10 to 12 minutes or until tender; let stand 5 minutes. Cut in half; remove seeds. Place cut side up in shallow glass baking dish; season with salt and pepper. Spoon hash into squash halves. Cook, covered with wax paper, on HIGH 4 to 5 minutes. Sprinkle with cheese; garnish with green pepper strips.*

Hash-Stuffed Peppers

- 4 green peppers
- 1 15-oz. can Armour Star Corned Beef Hash
- 2 slices process American cheese, cut in strips
- Stuffed green olive slices

Heat oven to 350°. Remove tops and seeds from green peppers. Cook in boiling salted water 5 minutes; drain. Spoon hash into peppers. Place in 8-inch square baking dish. Bake at 350°, 30 minutes. Top with cheese strips; heat 5 minutes or until cheese melts. Garnish with olive slices.

4 servings

Roast Turkey with Brown Rice Stuffing

- 1½ cups chopped celery
- 1 cup chopped onion
- ½ cup butter or margarine
- 3 cups quick brown rice, cooked
- 1 11-oz. can mandarin oranges, drained
- 1 cup raisins
- ½ cup slivered almonds
- 2 teaspoons salt
- ½ teaspoon thyme
- 1 12- to 14-lb. Armour Golden Star Young Turkey, thawed

Heat oven to 325°. In fry pan, cook celery and onion in butter or margarine 10 minutes; combine with remaining ingredients except turkey. Toss lightly. Loosely stuff neck and body cavities of turkey; roast according to label instructions. Place extra stuffing in greased 1½-quart casserole. Bake, covered, at 325°, 30 minutes.

12 cups stuffing

Roast Turkey with Easy Corn Stuffing

- 1 cup chopped onion
- ¾ cup butter or margarine
- 2 8-oz. packages corn bread stuffing
- 2 17-oz. cans whole kernel corn
- 2 2½-oz. jars sliced mushrooms
- 2 2¼-oz. cans sliced pitted ripe olives
- 1 12- to 14-lb. Armour Golden Star Young Turkey, thawed

Heat oven to 325°. Cook onion in butter or margarine 10 minutes; add remaining ingredients except turkey. Toss lightly. Loosely stuff neck and body cavities of turkey; roast according to label instructions. Place extra stuffing in greased 1½-quart casserole. Bake, covered, at 325°, 30 to 35 minutes.

8 cups stuffing

Roast Turkey 'n Corn Dressing

- 1 3- to 8-lb. Armour Golden Star Boneless Young Turkey, thawed
- ½ cup chopped onion
- ½ cup butter or margarine
- 1 6-oz. package corn bread dressing
- 1 17-oz. can whole kernel corn
- 1 2½-oz. jar sliced mushrooms
- 1 2¼-oz. can sliced pitted ripe olives

Heat oven to 350°. Roast turkey according to label instructions. While turkey is roasting, in fry pan, cook onion in butter or margarine 5 minutes; combine with remaining ingredients. Toss lightly; set aside. One hour before turkey is scheduled to be done, remove turkey from oven. Lift turkey and rack from pan. Scrape drippings from pan to use for gravy. Return turkey to pan without rack; turn turkey over. Brush turkey with some of reserved pan drippings. Spoon dressing into pan around turkey. Return to oven; continue roasting until done.

Turkey 'n Vegetable Roast

1 3- to 8-lb. Armour Golden Star Boneless Young Turkey, thawed
2 zucchini, sliced in 1-inch pieces
2 potatoes, peeled, quartered
2 onions, quartered
2 carrots, quartered

Heat oven to 350°. Roast turkey according to label instructions. One hour before turkey is scheduled to be done, remove turkey from oven. Place vegetables around turkey; baste with pan drippings. Return turkey and vegetables to 350° oven. Continue roasting, basting vegetables occasionally, until done.

Turkey Chow Mein

8 onion slices, separated into rings
2 cups sliced celery
2 tablespoons vegetable oil
1 16-oz. can bean sprouts, drained
2 cups chopped cooked Armour Golden Star Boneless Young Turkey
2 teaspoons Armour Star Chicken Flavor Instant Bouillon or 2 Armour Star Chicken Flavor Bouillon cubes dissolved in 1½ cups boiling water
2 tablespoons soy sauce
¼ teaspoon salt
Dash of pepper
2 tablespoons cornstarch
¼ cup cold water
Hot cooked rice
Chow mein noodles

In large fry pan, cook onion and celery in oil 10 minutes. Add bean sprouts, turkey and bouillon to fry pan; simmer 5 minutes. Add soy sauce, salt and pepper. Combine cornstarch with water; stir into mixture. Cook, stirring until thickened. Serve over rice. Garnish with noodles.

4 to 6 servings

Turkey 'n Vegetable Roast

Turkey Divan

- 12 slices cooked Armour Golden Star Young Turkey
- 2 10-oz. packages frozen asparagus spears, cooked according to package directions
- 1 10¾-oz. can cream of chicken soup
- ¾ cup (3 oz.) shredded Cheddar cheese

Heat oven to 375°. Arrange turkey in 10 × 6-inch baking dish; cover with asparagus. Pour on soup; sprinkle with cheese. Bake at 375°, 20 minutes.

6 servings

Fruited Turkey Kabobs

- 16 1-inch cubes cooked Armour Golden Star Boneless Young Turkey
- 8 orange segments
- 8 pear wedges
- 1 green pepper, cut in 12 1-inch squares
- 4 spiced crab apples
- ½ cup jellied cranberry sauce
- ½ cup apricot preserves
- ½ cup light corn syrup
- ¼ cup lemon juice
- 2 tablespoons butter or margarine
- ¼ teaspoon cinnamon
  Dash of cloves
  Hot cooked rice

Arrange turkey, orange, pear, green pepper and crab apples on four 10-inch metal skewers; place on broiler pan. In saucepan, combine remaining ingredients except rice; cook on medium heat, 5 minutes, stirring occasionally. Brush sauce on kabobs; broil 5 minutes on each side, turning and brushing occasionally with sauce. Serve on rice.

4 kabobs

Turkey-Noodle Scallop

- ½ cup chopped celery
- ¼ cup finely chopped onion
- ¼ cup butter or margarine
- ¼ cup flour
- ½ teaspoon salt
- Dash of white pepper
- Dash of poultry seasoning
- 1½ cups milk
- 1½ cups chicken broth
- 1 cup (4 oz.) shredded Cheddar cheese
- 1 tablespoon lemon juice
- 2 cups chopped cooked Armour Golden Star Young Turkey
- 2 cups hot cooked noodles
- ½ cup slivered almonds

Heat oven to 350°. Cook celery and onion in butter or margarine 10 minutes or until tender; blend in flour and seasonings. Gradually add milk and broth; cook, stirring constantly until thickened. Blend in cheese and lemon juice; stir in turkey and noodles. Pour into 2-quart casserole; top with almonds. Bake at 350°, 35 minutes.

6 servings

Sherried Turkey

- 1 package Armour Star Turkey Thighs
- ¼ cup butter or margarine
- 1 cup coarsely chopped onion
- 1 10¾-oz. can cream of mushroom soup
- ½ cup sherry
- Hot cooked rice

Heat oven to 325°. In fry pan, brown turkey in butter or margarine; remove to 2-quart casserole. Cook onion in remaining butter or margarine 5 minutes; stir in soup and sherry. Pour over turkey. Bake, covered, at 325°, 1 hour or until tender. Serve over rice.

4 servings

Turkey Tostados

- 4 corn tortillas
- 2 tablespoons vegetable oil, heated
- 1 15½-oz. can Armour Star Chili with Beans, heated
- 3 cups shredded lettuce
- 1 7-oz. can green chile salsa
- ½ cup (2 oz.) shredded Cheddar cheese
- 12 thin slices cooked Armour Golden Star Young Turkey
- 1 avocado, peeled, sliced
- Tomato wedges

Fry tortillas in oil until crisp; drain. Spread each with chili. Toss lettuce with ½ cup salsa; sprinkle on tortillas. Top with cheese, turkey, avocado and tomatoes. Serve with remaining salsa.

4 servings

Mexican Turkey Casserole

- 2 cups chopped cooked Armour Golden Star Boneless Young Turkey
- 1 10¾-oz. can cream of chicken soup
- 1 cup milk
- ¼ cup diced green chiles
- 2 cups crushed corn chips
- 1 cup chopped onion
- 1 cup (4 oz.) shredded Monterey Jack cheese
- 1 cup (4 oz.) shredded Cheddar cheese

Heat oven to 375°. In saucepan, combine turkey, soup, milk and chiles; heat slowly, stirring until bubbly. Sprinkle ⅓ of corn chips on bottom of 2-quart casserole; pour in ½ of turkey mixture, ½ cup onion and ½ cup of each cheese. Layer another ⅓ of corn chips, remaining turkey mixture, onion and cheeses; top with remaining corn chips. Bake at 375°, 45 minutes.

6 servings

Bavarian Baked Chicken

- 6 slices Armour Star Bacon
- 1 egg, slightly beaten
- 1½ cups milk
- 2 lbs. (3) chicken breasts, split
- 1 cup dry bread crumbs
- ¼ cup butter or margarine
- ¼ cup flour
- 1 teaspoon Armour Star Chicken Flavor Instant Bouillon or 1 Armour Star Chicken Flavor Bouillon cube dissolved in ½ cup boiling water
- 1½ cups (6 oz.) shredded Swiss cheese
- ½ teaspoon dill weed
- ½ teaspoon salt
- ¼ teaspoon pepper

Heat oven to 375°. In fry pan, cook bacon over medium heat until slightly crisp. Drain bacon, reserving drippings. Cut bacon in 1-inch pieces. Combine egg and ½ cup milk. Dip chicken in egg and milk mixture; roll in bread crumbs. In same fry pan, cook chicken over medium heat until golden brown on each side. Place chicken in 3-quart casserole. Bake, covered, at 375°, 30 minutes. In saucepan, melt butter or margarine over medium heat; stir in flour. Slowly add remaining milk, stirring until thickened. Add bouillon to pan; stir in cheese and seasonings. Cook over low heat until cheese melts. After chicken has baked 30 minutes, drain drippings. Reduce oven temperature to 325°. Pour sauce on chicken; top with bacon pieces. Bake, uncovered, at 325°, 20 minutes.

6 servings

Company's Coming

Fancy dishes for festive affairs: Remember when they were always hard work? Now, when company comes, you can feel like a guest yourself—Armour's done the work for you. Here are lots of delicious ideas that spare the cook and serve up plenty for any occasion. Buffets or birthdays. Suppers for a whole gang of video-football fans. Gala holiday gatherings, when the turkey or ham must be extra-special. These mouthwatering dishes will have everyone asking. "How can anything so good be *that* easy?"

Roast Turkey with Cranola Stuffing

- 1 teaspoon Armour Star Chicken Flavor Instant Bouillon or 1 Armour Star Chicken Flavor Bouillon cube dissolved in 1 cup boiling water
- 4 cups granola cereal
- 4 cups dry whole wheat bread cubes
- 3 cups coarsely chopped cranberries
- 1 cup chopped onion
- 4 eggs, beaten
- ½ cup chopped parsley
- 3 tablespoons grated lemon rind
- 2 teaspoons salt
- ½ teaspoon pepper
- 1 12- to 14-lb. Armour Golden Star Young Turkey, thawed

Heat oven to 325°. Combine all ingredients except turkey; toss lightly. Loosely stuff neck and body cavities of turkey; roast according to label instructions. Place extra stuffing in greased 2-quart casserole. Bake, covered, at 325°, 30 to 35 minutes.

12 cups stuffing

Roast Turkey with Olive-Rice Stuffing

  1½ cups chopped celery
  1 cup chopped onion
  ½ cup butter or margarine
  3 cups cooked quick brown rice
  1 cup sliced pitted ripe olives
  ½ cup sliced almonds
  2 teaspoons salt
  ½ teaspoon thyme
  1 12- to 14-lb. Armour Golden Star Young Turkey

Heat oven to 325°. In fry pan, cook celery and onion in butter or margarine 10 minutes; combine with remaining ingredients except turkey. Toss lightly. Loosely stuff neck and body cavities of turkey; roast according to label instructions. Place extra stuffing in greased 1½-quart casserole. Bake, covered, at 325°, 30 minutes.

12 cups stuffing

Roast Turkey with Triple Corn Stuffing

  1 lb. Armour Star Bacon
  1½ cups chopped celery
  ½ cup chopped onion
  1 12-oz. package (8 cups) corn bread dressing
  2 teaspoons poultry seasoning
  ½ teaspoon salt
  1 17-oz. can cream-style corn
  1 17-oz. can whole kernel corn
  1 12- to 14-lb. Armour Golden Star Young Turkey, thawed

Heat oven to 325°. In large fry pan, cook bacon until crisp; drain, reserving ⅓ cup drippings. Cut bacon in 1-inch pieces. In same fry pan, cook celery and onion in reserved drippings 10 minutes. Combine all ingredients except turkey; toss lightly. Loosely stuff neck and body cavities of turkey; roast according to label instructions. Place extra stuffing in 1½-quart casserole. Bake, covered, at 325°, 30 to 35 minutes.

10 cups stuffing

Roast Turkey with Apple-Yam Dressing

- 1 3- to 8-lb. Armour Golden Star Boneless Young Turkey, thawed
- 2 cups chopped apples
- ⅔ cup chopped onion
- ¾ cup butter or margarine
- 2 16-oz. cans yams, drained, mashed
- 2 tablespoons sugar
- 2 teaspoons salt
- ½ teaspoon nutmeg
- ½ teaspoon cinnamon
- 4 cups soft bread cubes

Heat oven to 350°. Roast turkey according to label instructions. While turkey is roasting, in fry pan, cook apples and onion in butter or margarine 10 minutes; combine with remaining ingredients. Toss lightly; set aside. One hour before turkey is scheduled to be done, remove turkey from oven. Lift turkey and rack from pan. Scrape drippings from pan to use for gravy. Return turkey to pan without rack; turn turkey over. Brush turkey with some of reserved pan drippings. Spoon dressing into pan around turkey. Return turkey and dressing to 350° oven; continue roasting until done.

Roast Turkey with Nutty Mushroom Stuffing

- 3 cups sliced mushrooms
- ½ cup chopped onion
- ½ cup snipped celery leaves
- ½ cup butter or margarine
- 6 cups cooked quick rice
- 1 cup chopped walnuts
- 2 teaspoons salt
- ½ teaspoon oregano leaves, crushed
- ½ teaspoon rubbed sage
- ½ teaspoon thyme leaves, crushed
- ¼ teaspoon pepper
- 1 12- to 14-lb. Armour Golden Star Young Turkey, thawed

Heat oven to 325°. In large fry pan, cook mushrooms, onion and celery leaves in butter or margarine 10 minutes. Stir in rice, walnuts and seasonings; heat through. Loosely stuff neck and body cavities of turkey; roast according to label instructions. Place extra stuffing in 1½-quart casserole. Bake, covered, at 325°, 30 to 35 minutes.

10 cups stuffing

Roast Turkey with Granola-Fruit Stuffing

  4 cups granola cereal
3½ cups cooked quick brown rice
  3 oranges, sectioned and chopped, reserving juice
  3 apples, peeled, cored and chopped
  1 cup raisins
  2 teaspoons salt
  1 teaspoon cinnamon
  1 cup chopped celery
  ¾ cup chopped onion
  ⅓ cup butter or margarine
  1 12- to 14-lb. Armour Golden Star Young Turkey, thawed

Heat oven to 325°. Combine cereal, rice, oranges and juice, apples, raisins, salt and cinnamon; set aside. In fry pan, cook celery and onion in butter or margarine 10 minutes. Add to cereal mixture; toss lightly. Loosely stuff neck and body cavities of turkey; roast according to label instructions. Place extra stuffing in greased 1½-quart casserole. Bake, covered, at 325°, 30 to 35 minutes.

12 cups stuffing

Roast Turkey with Oriental Almond Stuffing

- 1 cup finely chopped celery
- ½ cup finely chopped onion
- ½ cup butter or margarine
- 5 cups dry bread cubes
- 2 cups peeled, coarsely chopped apple
- 1 cup roasted sliced almonds
- 2 teaspoons grated orange rind
- ¼ cup orange juice
- 1 teaspoon salt
- ½ teaspoon thyme
- 1 12- to 14-lb. Armour Golden Star Young Turkey, thawed

Heat oven to 325°. Cook celery and onion in butter or margarine 10 minutes; add remaining ingredients except turkey. Toss lightly. Loosely stuff neck and body cavities of turkey; roast according to label instructions. Place extra stuffing in greased 1½-quart casserole. Bake, covered, at 325°, 30 to 35 minutes.

8 cups stuffing

Cranberry-Wine Sauce for Turkey

- 1 16-oz. can whole berry cranberry sauce
- ¼ cup Burgundy wine
- 2 tablespoons brown sugar, packed
- 1 tablespoon prepared mustard
- ¼ teaspoon onion salt
- Sliced cooked Armour Golden Star Young Turkey

In saucepan, combine all ingredients. Simmer, uncovered, 5 minutes. Serve warm or chilled with turkey.

2½ cups

Turkey Crêpes with Mornay Sauce

¼ cup chopped onion
6 tablespoons butter or margarine
2 cups chopped cooked Armour Golden Star Young Turkey
⅓ cup sliced pitted ripe olives
2 tablespoons chopped pimiento
½ teaspoon salt
　Pepper
¼ cup flour
2 cups milk
1 cup (4 oz.) shredded Swiss cheese
¼ cup grated Parmesan cheese
2 tablespoons chopped parsley
8 Crêpes (below)

Heat oven to 350°. Cook onion in 2 tablespoons butter or margarine 10 minutes or until tender. Stir in turkey, olives, pimiento, ¼ teaspoon salt and dash of pepper. Set aside. Melt remaining butter or margarine; blend in flour, ¼ teaspoon salt and dash of pepper. Gradually add milk; cook, stirring constantly until thickened. Blend in cheeses and parsley. Stir ½ cup cheese sauce into turkey mixture. Fill each crêpe with ¼ cup turkey mixture; roll. Place filled crêpes in greased 12 × 8-inch baking dish; cover with remaining sauce. Bake at 350°, 15 to 20 minutes.

4 servings

Crêpes: In medium mixing bowl, combine 2 eggs and dash salt. Gradually add 1 cup flour and 1 cup milk, beating until smooth. Beat in 2 tablespoons melted butter or margarine. Refrigerate batter at least 1 hour. For each crêpe, lightly brush 8-inch skillet with butter or margarine; heat on medium heat until butter or margarine is bubbly. Pour 3 to 4 tablespoons batter into skillet; immediately rotate pan until batter covers bottom. Cook until light brown; turn and brown on other side. Makes 16 to 18 crêpes.

Turkey Supreme

- ¼ cup chopped onion
- ¼ cup chopped celery
- 3 tablespoons butter or margarine
- 1 10¾-oz. can cream of mushroom soup
- ⅓ cup sherry
- 2 tablespoons chopped pimiento
- Dash of pepper
- 2 cups chopped cooked Armour Golden Star Young Turkey
- Hot cooked rice

Cook onion and celery in butter or margarine 5 minutes in saucepan. Add soup, sherry, pimiento and pepper; mix well. Stir in turkey. Heat thoroughly 10 minutes. Serve over rice.

4 servings

Zucchini-Turkey Bake

- 4 zucchini, cut in ½-inch slices
- ¾ cup sliced carrots
- Water
- ¼ teaspoon salt
- ½ cup chopped onion
- 6 tablespoons butter or margarine
- 2¼ cups seasoned stuffing cubes
- 2 cups cubed cooked Armour Golden Star Young Turkey
- 1 10¾-oz. can cream of chicken soup
- 1 cup dairy sour cream
- ½ cup grated Parmesan cheese

Heat oven to 350°. In covered saucepan, simmer zucchini and carrots in salted water to cover 15 minutes; drain. In large fry pan, cook onion in ¼ cup butter or margarine 10 minutes. Stir in 1½ cups stuffing cubes, turkey, soup and sour cream; gently fold in cooked vegetables. Pour mixture into greased 2-quart casserole. Top with remaining stuffing cubes and Parmesan cheese. Bake at 350°, 35 to 40 minutes.

6 to 8 servings

Rum-Raisin Glazed Ham

- 1 5- to 8-lb. Armour Star Boneless Ham
- 2 tablespoons brown sugar, packed
- 1 tablespoon cornstarch
- ½ cup water
- 1 cup raisins
- ½ cup orange juice
- ⅓ cup currant jelly
- ¼ teaspoon rum extract
  Dash of ground allspice
  Dash of salt

Heat ham according to label instructions. Combine brown sugar and cornstarch; gradually add water, stirring until well blended. Add remaining ingredients; cook, stirring occasionally, until thickened. Spoon over ham during last 30 minutes of heating.

Old-Fashioned Cherry Glazed Ham

- 1 3-lb. Golden Star Ham by Armour
- ¼ cup sugar
- 1 tablespoon cornstarch
- 1 16-oz. can red sour pitted cherries, drained, reserving liquid
- ½ teaspoon almond extract

Heat ham according to label instructions. Combine sugar and cornstarch in saucepan; gradually add reserved liquid. Cook, stirring constantly, over low heat until thickened; add cherries. Continue cooking until cherries are heated; stir in almond extract. Spoon over heated ham.

Frosted Easter Ham

- 1 8-oz. package cream cheese, softened
- ¼ cup plain yogurt
- 1 tablespoon lemon juice
- 1½ teaspoons prepared horseradish
- 1 teaspoon salt
- 1 5-lb. Armour Star Ham
- Shredded carrot
- Parsley sprigs
- Orange slices
- Radish roses

Combine cream cheese, yogurt, lemon juice, horseradish and salt. Beat with mixer until smooth. Remove excess gelatin from ham. Spread cream cheese mixture on top and sides of ham. Refrigerate several hours or overnight. Just before serving, garnish with carrot, parsley, orange slices and radish roses.

Ham Ambrosia

- 1 4- to 6-lb. Armour's 1877 Ham
- 1 8¼-oz. can crushed pineapple, drained
- 1 12-oz. jar orange marmalade
- ½ cup flaked coconut
- 2 tablespoons lemon juice

Heat ham according to label instructions. Combine remaining ingredients; spread over ham during last 30 minutes of heating.

Ham Galliano

- 1 5-lb. Golden Star Ham by Armour
- ¾ cup water
- 1 6-oz. can frozen orange juice concentrate, thawed
- ½ cup corn syrup
- ½ cup Liquore Galliano® liqueur

Heat oven to 325°. Place ham in shallow baking pan. Combine remaining ingredients; pour mixture over ham. Bake at 325°, 1 hour and 15 minutes to 1 hour and 30 minutes. Baste ham with sauce occasionally during heating time.

Lemon-Honey Glazed Ham

- 1 5- to 8-lb. Armour Star Boneless Ham
- 1 cup brown sugar, packed
- ¼ cup lemon juice
- ¼ cup honey
- 1 teaspoon dry mustard

Heat ham according to label instructions. Combine brown sugar, lemon juice, honey and dry mustard; bring to a boil, stirring occasionally. Spoon glaze over ham during last 15 minutes of heating time.

Ginger Ale Glazed Ham

- 1 5- to 8-lb. Armour Star Boneless Ham
- 1 cup brown sugar, packed
- ½ cup ginger ale
- ¼ teaspoon ginger
- ¼ teaspoon ground cloves

Heat ham according to label instructions. Combine remaining ingredients; spread over ham during last 30 minutes of heating.

Ham Roll-Ups

1 5-lb. Golden Star Ham by Armour
Lettuce leaves
Creamy Cucumber Sauce (below)
Mellow Horseradish Sauce (below)
Tangy Beet Relish (below)

Cut ham lengthwise into slices ¼-inch thick. Roll each slice; arrange on lettuce-lined platter. Serve with sauces.

CREAMY CUCUMBER SAUCE: Combine 1 3-oz. package softened cream cheese, ½ cup shredded cucumber, 1 teaspoon prepared horseradish, 1 teaspoon vinegar and ¼ teaspoon salt. Chill. Makes 1 cup sauce.

MELLOW HORSERADISH SAUCE: Combine 1 cup dairy sour cream, 2 teaspoons prepared horseradish, 1 teaspoon vinegar, ¼ teaspoon sugar, dash of Tabasco sauce and dash of salt. Chill. Makes 1 cup sauce.

TANGY BEET RELISH: In blender container, combine 1 16-oz. can drained cut beets, 2 tablespoons frozen orange juice concentrate, 1 tablespoon vinegar, 1 tablespoon chopped chives and ¼ teaspoon salt; blend at low speed until well mixed. Chill. Makes 1 cup relish.

Ham Romanoff

- 1 5- to 8-lb. Armour Star Boneless Ham
- ⅓ cup Russian dressing
- ½ cup brown sugar, packed
- ¼ teaspoon dry mustard

Heat ham according to label instructions. Combine remaining ingredients; spread over ham during last 30 minutes of heating.

Pork Roast with Apple Crowns

- 1 4- to 5-lb. Veribest Boneless Leg-O-Pork (Fresh Ham)
- 8 small apples, cored
- Orange juice
- ½ cup brown sugar, packed
- 2 tablespoons butter or margarine, melted
- 2 tablespoons chopped walnuts

Heat oven to 325°. Roast pork at 325° for 3 hours or until meat thermometer registers 170°. At midpoint of each apple, insert a sharp knife. Cut ½-inch diagonal points around apple, cutting to center. Carefully separate into halves; dip in orange juice. Place apples in 10 × 6-inch baking dish. Combine brown sugar, butter or margarine and walnuts; fill center of each apple with 1 tablespoon mixture. Bake at 325°, 35 to 40 minutes. Baste apples with glaze before serving.

6 to 8 servings

Apple Delite

- 1 2- to 2½-lb. Armour Star or 1877 Delite
- 1 medium cooking apple, cored, sliced into ¼-inch rings
- ½ cup red currant jelly
- ¼ cup brown sugar, packed

Heat oven to 325°. At ¾-inch intervals, slice Delite to ¼ inch from bottom. Place apple rings between slices. Place in 10 × 6-inch baking dish; bake at 325°, 1 hour and 20 minutes. In saucepan, heat jelly and brown sugar until well blended; brush on Delite during last 30 minutes of baking time.

8 servings

Microwave Instructions: *Prepare Delite as directed above. Place in 3-quart glass casserole. Cook, covered, on HIGH 15 to 20 minutes. Pour off liquid. Combine jelly and brown sugar in 1-quart glass casserole. Cook on HIGH 1 minute; stir halfway through heating time. Pour jelly mixture over Delite; cook, covered, on HIGH 3 minutes.*

Wilted Lettuce Salad with Bacon

- 1 quart torn Iceberg lettuce
- 1 quart torn Bibb lettuce
- ½ cup sliced radishes
- ⅓ cup sliced green onions
- 8 slices Armour Star Bacon
- ¼ cup sugar
- ¼ cup vinegar
- ½ teaspoon salt
- Dash of pepper

Combine lettuce, radishes and onions in a large salad bowl; toss lightly. Cook bacon until crisp; drain, reserving drippings. Crumble bacon; sprinkle over salad. Add remaining ingredients to drippings; bring to a boil over medium heat, stirring constantly. Pour over salad; toss lightly and quickly until lettuce wilts.

8 servings

Bacon Calico Combo

- 4 slices Armour Star Bacon
- 1 16-oz. can lima beans, drained
- 1 15-oz. can kidney beans, drained
- 1 15-oz. can garbanzo beans, drained
- 2 cups chopped onion
- 1 clove garlic, crushed
- ½ cup catsup
- 3 tablespoons brown sugar, packed
- 3 tablespoons vinegar
- 1 teaspoon dry mustard
- 1 teaspoon salt
- ¼ teaspoon pepper

In large fry pan, cook bacon until crisp. Remove from pan; crumble. Combine bacon and remaining ingredients in pan with bacon drippings. Heat, covered, over low heat 1 hour. Remove cover; stir. Continue heating uncovered, 30 minutes.

8 servings

Zippy Beef Barbecue

- ¼ cup flour
- 2 teaspoons salt
- ¼ teaspoon pepper
- 1 2-lb. Naturally Tender Beef Top Round Steak, cut into ⅛ × 3 inch strips
- ¼ cup vegetable oil
- ¾ cup water
- ½ cup chopped onion
- 1½ cups barbecue sauce
- ½ lb. mushrooms, sliced
- 8 hamburger buns, split

Combine flour, salt and pepper. Coat beef strips with flour mixture. In Dutch oven, cook beef on medium heat in oil 10 minutes. Add water and onion to beef; simmer, covered, 30 minutes. Add barbecue sauce and mushrooms; simmer, covered, 30 minutes, stirring occasionally. Serve on buns.

8 servings

Braised Beef 'n Vegetables

- 1 1½-lb. Naturally Tender Beef Bottom Round Steak, cut in ¼ × 3-inch strips
- 2 tablespoons vegetable oil
- 1 teaspoon salt
- ½ teaspoon thyme
- ¼ teaspoon pepper
- 1 teaspoon Armour Star Beef Flavor Instant Bouillon or 1 Armour Star Beef Flavor Bouillon cube dissolved in 1 cup boiling water
- 2 10-oz. packages frozen Italian green beans, thawed
- 2 cups sliced mushrooms
- ¾ cup buttermilk
- 1 tablespoon cornstarch
  Red onion rings
  Parsley sprigs

In large fry pan, cook beef on medium-high heat in oil 10 minutes; drain. Combine salt, thyme and pepper; sprinkle on beef. Add bouillon to beef; simmer, covered, 1 hour and 30 minutes. Stir in green beans and mushrooms; simmer, covered, 15 minutes. Combine buttermilk and cornstarch; gradually add to beef mixture. Cook over low heat, stirring until thickened. Garnish with onion and parsley.

4 servings

INDEX

Antipasto Appetizer Tray, 27
Appetizers, 26–47. *See also* Canapés; Dip(s); Spread(s).
Apple Delite, 152
Apple 'n Sauerkraut Sausage, 99
Apricot Pork Roast, 113

Bacon, 19
    Bacon-Avocado-Tomato Sandwich, 64
    Bacon-Bean Bake, 83
    Bacon Broil Sandwich, 70
    Bacon-Calico Combo, 153
    Bacon Cheesewich, 70
    Bacon Curls, 19
    Bacon-Macaroni Casserole, 108
    Bacon-Mushroom Crowns, 39
    Denver Bacon Brunch, 17
    Muffin-Cup Breakfast, 15
    Quiche Lorraine, 19
    Rumaki, 33
    Savory Stuffed Potatoes, 109
    Spaghetti alla Carbonara, 112
    Soufflé Lorraine, 17
    Wilted Lettuce Salad with Bacon, 152
Bavarian Baked Chicken, 135
Beans
    Bacon-Bean Bake, 83
    Bacon-Calico Combo, 153
    Easy Barbecue Bean Bake, 83
    Pantry-Shelf Casserole, 107
Beef. *See also* Chili; Corned beef; Dried beef; Sloppy Joes; Steak; Stew.
    Braised Beef 'n Vegetables, 155
    Hawaiian Beef Kabobs, 91
    Pizza Loaf, 77
    Zucchini-Beef Bake, 144
    Zippy Beef Barbecue, 153
Bologna
    Campfire Picnic Buns, 76
    Crunchy Cranberry Sandwich, 61
    Peanut Butter-Bologna Grill, 69
    Skyscraper, 60
    Tasty 'Tater Tidbits, 41
    The Works, 66
Breakfast Steak Diane, 23
Breakfast Stroganoff, 22
Broccoli Crêpes, Saucy, 94
Brown-Bagger Basic, 68

Campfire Picnic Buns, 76
Canapés. *See also* Spread(s).
    Chile-Ham, 28
    Party-Pleasers, 29
    South-of-the-Border Viennas, 33
Cheesy Corned Beef-Cabbage Casserole, 125
Cheesy Meat Spread, 44
Cheesy Open-Face Sandwich, 68
Chef's Sandwich, 64
Chicken, Bavarian Baked, 135
Chile-Ham Canapés, 28
Chili
    Chili-Cheese Dip, Hot, 43
    Chili Dogs, 75
    Chili Omelet, 11
    Chili-Onion Cups, 40
    Chili Plus, 82
    Chili Strata, 120
    Chili-Stuffed Zucchini, 124
    Chili Weather Peppers, 81
    Fireside Chili Pot, 82
Chow Mein, Turkey, 131
Chowder. *See also* Soup.
    Potato-Dried Beef, 86
    Vienna Sausage-Corn, 85
Chuck Wagon Steak, 121
Coney Island Hot Dogs, 75
Confetti Cottage Cheese, 57
Corned Beef
    Cheesy Corned Beef-Cabbage Casserole, 125
    Corned Beef and Cabbage, 124
    Corned Beef Meltaways, 72
    Irish Mac Salad, 59
    Reuben Melt, 72
Corned beef hash
    Corned Beef O'Brien, 21
    Corn-Hash Muffins, 84
    Hash 'n Squash, 126
    Hash Patties, 80
    Hash Pie, 126
    Hash-Stuffed Peppers, 128
    Shamrock Pie, 32
Cottage Cheese-Beef Spread, 35
Cottage Cheese, Confetti, 57
Country Vegetable Sandwich, 59
Cranberry Sandwich, Crunchy, 61
Cranberry-Wine Sauce for Turkey, 142
Cream Puffs, Ham-Filled, 28
Creamed Eggs and Beef, 21

Crêpes
    Saucy Broccoli, 94
    Turkey, with Mornay Sauce, 143
Curried Turkey-Fruit Salad, 52

Deli Sandwich, 66
Delite à l'Orange, 112
Denver Bacon Brunch, 17
Deviled Dogs, 76
Deviled Ham Dip, 47
Devilish Meat and Egg Sandwich, 60
Dip(s). See also Spread(s).
    Baked Beef, 38
    Creamy Beef, 44
    Deviled Ham, 47
    Hot Chili-Cheese, 43
Dried beef
    Baked Beef Dip, 38
    Beef à la Reine, 94
    Beef and Mushroom Quiche, 20
    Beef and Tangy 'Taters, 93
    Beef 'n Cheese Nut Log, 37
    Beef 'n Mac Casserole, 123
    Beef Romanoff, 93
    Beefy Cheese Ball, 37
    Cottage Cheese-Beef Spread, 35
    Creamed Eggs and Beef, 21
    Creamy Beef Dip, 44
    Creamy Beef Roll-Ups, 32
    Mock Monte Cristo Sandwich, 22
    Potato-Dried Beef Chowder, 86
    "Say Cheese" Rarebit, 24
    Scrambled Eggs Deluxe, 12
    Spinach-Beef Spread, 36

Eggs
    Chili Omelet, 11
    Creamed Eggs and Beef, 21
    Crunchy Breakfast Eggs, 14
    Denver Bacon Brunch, 17
    Deviled Eggs, Meaty, 43
    Devilish Meat and Egg Sandwich, 60
    Eggs Benedict, 16
    Hot Dog Breakfast Hash, 15
    Mexicali Eggs, 16
    Muffin-Cup Breakfast, 15
    Salami Breakfast Eggs, 14
    Scrambled Eggs Deluxe, 12
    Soufflé Lorraine, 17
    Sunrise Star, 13

Far East Beef Stew, 118
Fireside Chili Pot, 82
Florentine Chopped Ham, 90

Franks. See also Hot Dogs.
    Franks 'n Hot Potato Salad, 105
    Franks 'n Kraut Goulash, 105
    Spicy Cantonese Appetizers, 45
    Taco Franks, 81
Fritters, Ham, 116
Frosted Easter Ham, 147
Fruited Turkey Kabobs, 132

Garden-Variety Pizza, 78
Ginger Ale Glazed Ham, 149
Gondolier's Sandwich, 61
Griddle Cakes, Ham, 26

Ham(s)
    about, 9
    Ambrosia, 147
    Frosted Easter, 147
    Galliano, 148
    Ginger Ale Glazed, 148
    Lemon-Honey Glazed, 148
    Magic Cherry, 116
    Mincemeat-Glazed, 114
    Old-Fashioned Cherry Glazed, 145
    Orange Blossom, 117
    Plum Nuts, 114
    Romanoff, 150
    Rum-Raisin Glazed, 145
Ham appetizers
    Chile-Ham Canapés, 28
    Creamy Ham Spread, 36
    Deviled Ham Dip, 47
    Festive Ham Apple-tizers, 45
    Glazed Ham Bits, 46
    Ham-Filled Cream Puffs, 28
    Ham 'n Cheese Nut Log, 35
    Ham Scallops with Mustard Dip, 47
    Mushrooms Elegant, 40
Ham dishes
    Chef's Sandwich, 64
    Crunchy Garden-Ham Bake, 91
    Eggs Benedict, 16
    Florentine Chopped Ham, 90
    Ham and Waffles Jubilee, 23
    Ham Fritters, 116
    Ham Griddle Cakes, 24
    Ham Roll-Ups, 149
    Peach-Glazed Ham Loaf, 117
    Sunrise Star, 13
Ham salads
    Ham Confetti Mousse, 53
    Ham-Macaroni Salad, 54
    Ham-Orange Salad, 53
    Ham Waldorf Salad, 56

Hash 'n Squash, 126
Hash Patties, 80
Hash Pie, 126
Hash-Stuffed Peppers, 128
Hawaiian Beef Kabobs, 91
Hawaiian Salad, 49
Hot dogs. *See also* Franks.
  Chili Dogs, 75
  Coney Island Hot Dogs, 75
  Deviled Dogs, 76
  Family Hot Dog Supper, 102
  Glazed Hot Dog Dunkers, 40
  Hot Dog Breakfast Hash, 15
  Hot Dog Crescents, 101
  Hot Dog-Raisin Roll-Ups, 25
  Hot Dog Splits, 102
  Joe's Dogs, 75
  Orange-Nut Buns, 25

Irish Mac Salad, 59

Jambalaya, New Orleans, 110
Joe's Dogs, 75

Kabobs
  Fruited Turkey, 132
  Hawaiian Beef, 91
  Tangy, 107
Kraut-Wurst Sandwich, 73
Kulbassy-Potato Combo, 99

Leftover-Magic Turkey Stack, 62
Lemon-Honey Glazed Ham, 148
Lunch(eon) meat. *See also*
    Bologna; Salami; Treet.
  Beef 'n Cheese Strata, 121
  Country Vegetable Sandwich, 59
  Deli Sandwich, 66
  Easy Barbecue Bean Bake, 83
  Hawaiian Salad, 49
  Open-Face Summer Sandwich, 67
  Saucy Fiesta, 88
  Skyscraper, 60
  Southern Hospitality Rolls, 30

Macaroni
  Bacon-Macaroni Casserole, 108
  Beef 'n Macaroni Casserole, 123
  Family Hot Dog Supper, 102
  Ham-Macaroni Salad, 54
  Irish Mac Salad, 59
  Smackaroni Salad, 57
  Vegetable Patch Salad, 54
Meaty Deviled Eggs, 43

Mexicali Eggs, 16
Mexican Stack-Ups, 125
Mexican Turkey Casserole, 134
Mincemeat-Glazed Ham, 115
Mock Monte Cristo Sandwich, 22
Mousse, Ham Confetti, 53
Muffin-Cup Breakfast, 15
Muffin, Corn-Hash, 84
Mushroom, Bacon-, Crowns, 39
Mushroom and Beef Quiche, 20
Mushrooms Elegant, 40

New England Sausage Dinner, 97
New Orleans Jambalaya, 110

Old English Potted Meat Spread, 38
Omelet, Chili, 11
Open-Face Summer Sandwich, 67
Orange, Ham-, Salad, 53
Orange Blossom Ham, 117
Orange Blossom Sandwich, 67
Orange-Nut Buns, 25
Oriental Turkey Soup, 86

Pantry-Shelf Casserole, 107
Party-Pleasers, 29
Paul Bunyan Sausage Supper, 100
Peach-Glazed Ham Loaf, 117
Peanut Butter-Bologna Grill, 69
Peperoni Pizza, 78
Peppers, Chili Weather, 81
Peppers, Hash-Stuffed, 128
Picadilly Sandwich, 69
Pizza(s)
  Garden-Variety, 78
  Individual Taco, 29
  Peperoni, 78
  Shamrock Pie, 32
Pizza Loaf, 77
Plum Nuts Ham, 115
Pork. *See also* Bacon; Franks; *ham*
    entries; Hot dogs; Lunch(eon)
    meat; Sausage(s); Sloppy
    Joes; Treet; Vienna sausage.
  Apple Delite, 152
  Apricot Pork Roast, 113
  Delite à l'Orange, 112
  Creamy Split Pea Soup, 85
  New Orleans Jambalaya, 110
  Pork Roast with Apple Crowns, 150
  Roast Leg-O-Pork with Potato
    Medley, 113
  Scalloped Delite, 90
  Stuffed Pork Chops, 109

Potatoes
 Beef and Tangy 'Taters, 93
 Easy Skillet Scallop, 108
 Family Hot Dog Supper, 102
 Franks 'n Hot Potato Salad, 105
 Hot Dog Breakfast Hash, 15
 Kulbassy-Potato Combo, 99
 Paul Bunyan Sausage Supper, 100
 Potato-Dried Beef Chowder, 86
 Savory Stuffed Potatoes, 109
 Scalloped Delite, 90
 Skillet Sausage Sweets, 101
 Sloppy Joes Potatoes, 123
 Tasty 'Tater Tidbits, 41
Potted Meat
 Cheesy Meat Spread, 44
 Devilish Meat and Egg Sandwich, 60
 Meaty Deviled Eggs, 43
 Party-Pleasers, 29
 Spread, Old English, 38
 Tangy Spread, 35

Quiche
 Beef and Mushroom, 20
 Lorraine, 19
 Swiss Yodeler Pie, 20
 Turkey, 88

Rarebit
 Saucy Fiesta, 91
 "Say Cheese," 24
 Viennese, 89
Reuben Melt, 72
Rice, Sausage Fried, 110
Rum-Raisin Glazed Ham, 145
Rumaki, 33

Sailor's Stew, 77
Salad(s), 48–59
 Potato, Hot, Franks 'n, 105
 Wilted Lettuce, with Bacon, 152
Salami
 Antipasto Appetizer Tray, 27
 Brown-Bagger Basic, 68
 Chef's Sandwich, 64
 Confetti Cottage Cheese, 57
 Golden Salami Grill, 73
 Gondolier's Sandwich, 61
 Orange Blossom Sandwich, 67
 Salami Breakfast Eggs, 14
 Savory Salami Wedges, 30
 Smackaroni Salad, 57
 Swiss Salami Salad, 56
 The Works, 66

Sandwiches, 59–77
 Mock Monte Cristo Sandwich, 22
 Zippy Beef Barbecue, 153
Sausage(s). *See also* Franks; Hot
  dogs; Salami; Vienna sausage.
 Apple 'n Sauerkraut Sausage, 99
 Breakfast Stroganoff, 22
 Crunchy Breakfast Eggs, 14
 Gondolier's Sandwich, 61
 Kraut-Wurst Sandwich, 73
 Kulbassy-Potato Combo, 99
 New England Sausage Dinner, 97
 Paul Bunyan Sausage Supper, 100
 Peperoni Pizza, 78
 Sausage Bits with Mustard Dip, 46
 Skillet Sausage Sweets, 101
 Spaghetti-Sausage Supper, 100
Sausage Fried Rice, 110
"Say Cheese" Rarebit, 24
Saucy Fiesta, 91
Scalloped Delite, 90
Scrambled Eggs Deluxe, 12
Shamrock Pie, 32
Sherried Turkey, 133
Skillet Sausage Sweets, 101
Skyscraper, 60
Sloppy Joes
 Joe's Dogs, 75
 Sloppy Joes Olé, 80
 Sloppy Joes Potatoes, 123
Smackaroni Salad, 57
Soufflé Lorraine, 17
Soup. *See also* Chowder.
 Creamy Split Pea, 85
 Oriental Turkey, 86
 Tangy Cream of Spinach, 84
South-of-the-Border Viennas, 33
Southern Hospitality Rolls, 30
Spaghetti alla Carbonara, 112
Spaghetti-Sausage Supper, 100
Split Pea Soup, Creamy, 85
Spinach-Beef Spread, 36
Spinach Soup, Cream of, Tangy, 84
Spread(s)
 Beef 'n Cheese Nut Log, 37
 Beefy Cheese Ball, 37
 Cheesy Meat, 44
 Cottage Cheese-Beef, 35
 Ham, Creamy, 36
 Ham 'n Cheese Nut Log, 35
 Old English Potted Meat, 38
 Spinach-Beef, 36
 Tangy, 35
Squash, Hash 'n, 126

159

Steak
   Breakfast Steak Diane, 23
   Chuck Wagon Steak, 121
Stew
   Beef Stew with Parsley Dumplings, 120
   Far East Beef Stew, 118
   Sailor's Stew, 77
   Stew 'n Corn Bread Casserole, 118
Stuffed Pork Chops, 109
Stuffings. See Turkey, roast.
Sunrise Star, 13
Swiss Salami Salad, 56
Swiss Yodeler Pie, 20

Taco Franks, 81
Taco Pizzas, Individual, 29
The Works, 66
Tostados, Turkey, 134
Treet
   Easy-Time Sandwich, 62
   Garden-Variety Pizza, 78
   Mexicali Eggs, 16
   Pantry-Shelf Casserole, 107
   Picadilly Sandwiches, 69
   Swiss Yodeler Pie, 20
   Tangy Kabobs, 107
Turkey, roast
   about, 8–9
   'n Corn Dressing, 129
   Turkey 'n Vegetable Roast, 131
   with Apple-Yam Dressing, 139
   with Brown Rice Stuffing, 128
   with Cranola Stuffing, 137
   with Easy Corn Stuffing, 129
   with Granola-Fruit Stuffing, 141
   with Nutty Mushroom Stuffing, 140
   with Olive-Rice Stuffing, 138
   with Oriental Almond Stuffing, 142
   with Triple Corn Stuffing, 138

Turkey dishes
   Cranberry-Wine Sauce for Turkey, 142
   Fruited Turkey Kabobs, 132
   Hot Crunchy Turkey Cups, 88
   Leftover-Magic Turkey Stack, 62
   Mexican Turkey Casserole, 134
   Oriental Turkey Soup, 86
   Sherried Turkey, 133
   Turkey Chow Mein, 131
   Turkey Crêpes with Mornay Sauce, 143
   Turkey Divan, 132
   Turkey-Noodle Scallop, 133
   Turkey Quiche, 88
   Turkey Supreme, 144
   Turkey Tostados, 134
   Zucchini-Turkey Bake, 144
Turkey salads
   Apple-Turkey Toss, 51
   Curried Turkey-Fruit Salad, 52
   Tempting Turkey Salad, 52
   Turkey-Fruit Toss, 51

Vegetable-Patch Salad, 54
Vienna sausage
   Crispy Barbecue Bites, 41
   Sausage Fried Rice, 110
   South-of-the-Border Viennas, 33
   Vegetable-Patch Salad, 54
   Vienna Biscuit Ring, 89
   Vienna Sausage-Corn Chowder, 85
   Viennese Rarebit, 89

Waffles, Ham and, Jubilee, 23
Wilted Lettuce Salad with Bacon, 152

Zucchini, Chili-Stuffed, 124
Zucchini-Beef Bake, 92
Zucchini-Turkey Bake, 144